In the Gladness of Today

In the Gladness of Today

Thoughts for the Day

RICHARD HARRIES

Fount

An Imprint of HarperCollins*Publishers*

Fount is an Imprint of
HarperCollins*Religious*
Part of HarperCollins*Publishers*
77–85 Fulham Palace Road, London W6 8JB

First published in Great Britain in 1999 by Fount

1 3 5 7 9 10 8 6 4 2

A catalogue record for this book is
available from the British Library

ISBN 0 00 628149 4

Printed and bound in Great Britain by
Caledonian International Book Manufacturing Ltd, Glasgow

For Luke Richard Harries

CONTENTS

INTRODUCTION

IT IS A GREAT PRIVILEGE TO TALK TO MILLIONS OF PEOPLE at 7.48 a.m. on the *Today* programme. It is also very difficult. Although I have been doing regular religious slots on the programme since 1972, it does not get any easier. First, what one says has to be related to the current news in some way. Yet at the same time it needs to avoid being either political or platitudinous. Furthermore, the talk has to have a theological dimension that is accessible to people of many faiths and none, who are half listening as they go off the work, eat breakfast or clean their teeth.

I find it helps if I can use some poetry. This is because I like to share good things I have come across with other people. But, even more important, the words of a poem may represent a lifetime's distilled thought and experience. They are more likely to have some enduring value than anything conjured out of a pressured Bishop's life in a couple of hours.

The routine for a 'Thought' involves ringing the producer at the BBC's Religious Broadcasting Department (now based in Manchester) on the day before to discuss possible subjects. It cannot be prepared before that because news, of its nature, either passes or becomes different. Then, perhaps in the evening, the script is written and read through to the producer. So I would like to pay tribute to the producers who over the years have heard my scripts and have often made helpful suggestions. Sometimes, because a major story breaks during the night, a new script has to be written at short notice. For example, I was given two hours to write one in response to the death of Princess Diana. I would like to thank the *Today* team for their friendliness and courtesy. They may give politicians a hard time, but their warm verbal welcome to those doing a 'Thought for the Day' makes us feel very much part of the programme.

I am glad to make a new collection of my 'Thoughts' available in print. Originally they were written in response to current news stories, but I also hope that they will be of some continuing help to those who are open to the spiritual dimension of life.

✠ Richard Oxon
June 1999

ALL CREATION REJOICES IN THEE

GRAVITY AND WAGGERY

RASTUS IS DEAD. I NEVER KNEW HIM, BUT I COULDN'T MISS the picture in yesterday's newspaper. His back paws were on the petrol tank of an old motorbike, his front ones on the handlebars, body leaning forward. Rastus – a cat who had been rescued by a biker – rode this way for hundreds of thousands of miles, his helmet matching that of his owner, raising money for charity and creating his own fan club. Sadly, one day in New Zealand they ran into a car coming the other way, and that was the end of both of them.

I would not have noticed the picture except that in recent months my daughter's cat has been staying with us. She also was rescued, and very nervous she is too, no doubt as a result of early traumas. But she's settling in, and there are some good moments. First thing in the morning, for example, Kitty eats just a little of her food and then comes into my study for one of her rare, graciously bestowed purrs. Whilst I do some meditative reading she sits and murmurs on my lap. We are fellow creatures – and what a mystery we are to each other. I suspect that Ted Hughes has been so appreciated in recent years because, as much as any poet, he has caught the sense of otherness, the strangeness, the mystery of the animal world.

One of the recovered insights of our time is a respect for animals in their own right. They are not just there to be of use to us, though that is part of the Christian tradition. They have significance in themselves as part of the sheer exuberance and the fantastic richness and variety of creation. Yet it is not so much the poetry of Ted Hughes that comes to my mind when I look at Kitty, or even T. S. Eliot's poems about cats that were made into a musical. It is poor Christopher Smart, the eighteenth-century poet who spent years of his adult life in Bedlam lunatic asylum. He, like so many of the rest of us, found consolation in his cat. Indeed, he wrote a poem about him:

For I will consider my cat Jeoffry.
For he is the servant of the living God duly and daily serving him.
For at the first glance of the glory of God in the East
　　he worships in his way.
For is this done by wreathing his body seven times round
　　with elegant quickness.
For then he leaps up to catch the musk,
　　which is the blessing of God upon his prayer...

And so on through all the things that Jeoffry does in the morning and at night – more than 1,500 lines, and that's only the fragments that remain. He was doing his thing, praising God in his way. As Smart put it:

For his is a mixture of gravity and waggery
For he knows that God is his Saviour.

NOTHING BUT MIRACLES

16 July 1998

SOME COMPANY EXECUTIVES WERE RECENTLY PERSUADED to walk on red-hot coals. Not surprisingly, they badly burnt their feet and had to be rushed to hospital. A bizarre training exercise that went badly wrong. The trainers wanted their business whizz-kids to show that mind could conquer matter, that with the right mental attitude they could overcome fear. Some clearly succeeded. One man reported that he had a framed certificate saying that he had 'performed the miraculous.' But in my book far more miraculous is the fact that our feet can feel pain and send message to the brain, which in turn can send messages back to the feet to jump off those coals quickly. The ordinary capacities which help us to survive are far more wondrous than any stunts.

A story that went round the Commons has two Labour MPs looking out of the window across the Thames, when they suddenly see Tony Blair walking on water. One of them – of the recalcitrant old Labour school – blurted out in language that I have to tone down, 'Look at him – the b —— can't even swim!' Making a rather different point to that MP, I would want to say that our human capacity to swim, in the widest sense – to adapt to an environment and make it work to our benefit – is more amazing than any strange phenomenon.

My wife and I have just had the delight of another grandchild. We were shown pictures of a tiny babe in the womb and now here he is – the product of 13 billion years of the universe's evolution and many millions of years of biological evolution on this planet. He sums up in himself what has gone before in literally miraculous complexity – for example, there are 100 billion neurones in his brain poised to receive information. All this has been achieved by atoms and cells going on being themselves in those observed regularities that we call 'laws of nature'. If the Psalmist 3,000 years ago could say, 'I will give thanks unto thee, for I am fearfully and wonderfully made', how much more can we echo that today. In those so-called ordinary things that we take for granted – the light shining in the window, the kettle boiling for tea, the oxygen we breathe, the rhythms and regularities by which we live and on the basis of which we plan our lives – is reflected the faithfulness of our creator. So I agree with the poet Walt Whitman when he wrote:

As to me I know nothing else but miracles
Whether I walk the streets of Manhattan,
Or dart my sight over the roofs of houses towards the sky.

The Good Soil

3 November 1997

CHERIE BLAIR HAS REVEALED THAT THE DEFINING MOMENT in her life came when she was nine years old. Her parents had divorced and her school studies were suffering. Then a perceptive teacher who recognized her potential, realized that she needed a challenge. So he persuaded her mother to allow her to go up a class. It proved a great success and, as Cherie Blair has put it, 'I often think that I owed my later success to that teacher.'

I once visited an adult-learning class in Oxford and spoke to a late-middle-aged man who was learning to read with the aid of a computer. All his life he had worked in a factory and then suddenly he was made redundant. He went to a Job Centre, joined the queue and was told by the person at the counter to read the job vacancies. He couldn't. He told me that when he had been at school there had been such a rapid change of teachers that he had never managed to get into reading. And large numbers of other people are in the same position as that man.

Unlike him and like Cherie Blair, I was one of the lucky ones. At an important stage in my school career a teacher came into my life who believed in me, who thought I had potential for something.

Too often today teachers get a bad press – most unfairly, I think. For they are being asked to pick up the pieces of a lawless, selfish society which has been deeply wounded by family breakdown. In some schools it's a very testing job indeed. In D. H. Lawrence's novel *The Rainbow* Ursula Brangwen starts as a teacher with such high hopes. As Lawrence writes, 'She would make everything personal and vivid, she would give herself, she would give, give, give all her great stores and wealth to her children, she would make them so happy.' But all too soon she felt totally crushed. As Lawrence put it, she was 'rebuffed, troubled by the new atmosphere, out of place'. No school today is as bad as the one she went to, thank goodness, but still the most idealistic teacher can become distraught and disillusioned by the problems that our society unloads in the classroom.

At such times of difficulty it is good to think of one of the most famous stories of Jesus. Some seed fell along the footpath, some fell on rocky ground, some fell among thistles – all wasted, yes – but the climax of the parable and its point is the fact that some seed fell into good soil where it yielded thirtyfold, sixtyfold, even a hundredfold. It's that ultimate optimism of Jesus that I find so appealing. For it means that all the unknown good we do, probably long forgotten even by us, will in the end flower in surprising ways and unexpected places.

SPRAWL

30 July 1993

MIKE ATHERTON CLEARLY PLEASED THE PRESS AT HIS FIRST interview after taking over as the captain of the England cricket team. As one commentator wrote: 'He is clever, but no clever-clogs; a smiler, but not smarmy; confident, never cocky.'

He will certainly need all that inner equilibrium, not only to take England's cricket out of the doldrums but to cope with the pressure of the job. It's a quality that is vividly depicted in one of my favourite poems, by the Australian writer Les Murray. It's called, rather surprisingly, 'The Quality of Sprawl', but what he is concerned about is how a person can do their own thing, sometimes in quite outrageous ways, without simply doing it to show off. He begins:

Sprawl is the quality
of the man who cut down his Rolls Royce
into a farm utility truck, and sprawl
is what the company lacked when it made repeated efforts
to buy the vehicle back and repair its image.

Murray goes on to describe, in a series of contrasts in sport, the arts and history, how this quality reveals itself and where it is absent. There's nothing prim and proper about it. 'Sprawl is really classless', he writes.

It's John Christopher Frederick Murray
Asleep in his neighbours' best bed in spurs and oilskins
but not having thrown up.

I think that St Paul also struggled with the problem of how to overcome the desire to impress others all the time, whether other people or God; with how to get together as a person, so that we can be our own man or woman. He came to believe that we come together as a person when we come together with Christ; that we become our own person, if we are fully God's first. This is what he meant by the rather technical theological phrase, 'We are justified by grace, through faith.' We awake to the fact that we have our own worth in ourself, for ourself.

There are hints in Murray's poem that he also shares this view. One line reads, 'It is the rococo of being your own still centre.'

There is a relaxed quality about 'sprawl', and therefore, as Murray says, it gets up the nose of many kinds of people. But that relaxedness has a toughness that is rooted elsewhere. The poem ends:

Reprimanded and dismissed
it listens with a grin and one boot up on the rail
of possibility. It may have to leave the earth.
Being roughly Christian, it scratches the other cheek
and thinks it unlikely.
Though people have been shot for sprawl.

We all need time to do a bit of sprawling; both relaxing and discovering that inner calm and strength. For it is this which enables us to withstand the pressures of life, and to be our own person.

LAUGHTER

12 March 1993

WHEN COMMUNISM WAS COLLAPSING IN THE SOVIET UNION, it was said that the Communist Party offered a reward of 50 roubles for everyone who renewed their subscription. Furthermore, if you persuaded someone else to join the Party, not only did you get the 50 roubles, but you yourself were allowed to leave. As a final bonus, if you persuaded two people to sign up, not only were you allowed to leave, but you received a certificate saying that you never were a member of the Party!

Today in Moscow, as the constitutional crisis deepens and goes into its third day, there will be much more of this black humour. Today in Britain, Comic Relief will channel good humour into a good cause. But for the Russians jokes are an essential tool in their survival kit.

Some humour is very close to despair. It is well known that behind the comic faces and loud laughter of some famous comedians there lurks a profound melancholy. Precisely for this reason I think that humour is often an act of courage. It expresses a determination not to let 'them' get you down –

whoever 'they' are – and not to be ground down by life. That's why people who have suffered a lot – not only the Russians but also the Jews and the Irish – developed such a wonderful sense of humour. Time and again they have faced the stark choice of letting circumstances crush them or defying them with a joke.

This means, I think, that we cannot finally rest with humour alone. It is a kind of halfway house between despair and faith. For either it is a wonderfully brave gesture over a pit of meaninglessness, or it is a kind of anticipation of the triumph of love over evil. Humour finds its fulfilment in faith.

Today there will, I hope, be plenty of good humour and cheerful laughter – and all in a good cause. But there are many kinds of laughter. As Harry Williams once put it in a memorable sentence, 'Is it to go on always like now, just – tomorrow and tomorrow and tomorrow – a slow procession of dusty greyish events with a lot of forced laughter, committee laughter, cocktail laughter and streaks of downright pain?' The pain is part of life and that pain can be disguised by some kinds of laughter. But real, deep, genuine laughter can be not only a brave gesture of defiance but also an echo of love's victory.

There's a sentence in the Psalms that I have never been happy with. It depicts God laughing at the forces of evil: 'He that dwelleth in heaven shall laugh them to scorn.' But if this is the laughter that echoed amongst the Jews, helping them to survive persecution down the ages, and amongst the Russians standing up to Communism, I want to go along with it.

THE WORLD'S HIGH PRIEST

4 October 1991

A WHILE AGO MY WIFE AND I WENT FOR A WALK IN THE Cotswolds. At one point the view across field and hill was quite fabulous – and the smell was appalling! Nearby was a vast, black, windowless building. We averted not only our noses but our eyes. We did not want to think too much about the animals inside.

There is no doubt that in some ways we are more sensitive to animal suffering than previous generations were. When I attended a conference for sixth formers a while ago I noticed that a good percentage of them were vegetarians. This is, I suspect, true of young people generally. Yet there is still gross neglect and cruelty about. The churches are sometimes blamed for complacency about this because of a wrong attitude to animals. The culprit is held to be Genesis 1:26, which, after asserting that human beings are created in the image of God, goes on to say: 'And let them have dominion over the fish of the sea, and over the birds of the air, and over the cattle, and over all the earth.'

The use of that word 'dominion' has sometimes led people to think that we can do what we like with animals. But just the opposite is true. Our attitude to them, according to the text, is set firmly within the context of being made in the image of God. In short, our relationship to the animal world is meant to reflect God's caring relationship to us.

Although some Christian thinking about animals has been harsh, there has also been a much more positive tradition, which emerged, for example, in the seventeenth-century Anglican priest and poet, George Herbert. In his poem 'Providence' he writes:

Man is the world's high priest: he doth present
the sacrifice for all; while they below
Unto the service mutter an assent.

Humanity is 'the world's high priest' – that is, we are bound up with the animals, our fellow creatures, but we are able to articulate that world in prayer and praise to God.

Dominion, then, is to be expressed in terms of priesthood. Some people, like St Francis, clearly have a real affinity with animals. Most of us enjoy the companionship of cats, dogs and other domesticated creatures and are enthralled by wildlife. There is much here for which to give thanks and praise. But priesthood also means a proper respect for the animal world, and that will involve putting right those current practices which inflict avoidable suffering on animals – carting lifestock to the Continent in confined spaces, for example, and some factory farms which restrict the movement of beasts or birds in unacceptable ways. You do not have to be sentimental, cranky or fanatical to care about animals. As human beings it is part of our fundamental responsibility as 'the world's high priest'.

THE SCORPION

26 June 1991

THIS COMING SUNDAY IS THE ONE HUNDREDTH ANNIVER-
sary of the birth of the painter Stanley Spencer. Cookham, the
village in Berkshire where he lived all his life, will be celebrat-
ing. For it was there that he painted the landscapes which
earned his bread and butter and the major visionary paintings
with which he is associated, *Christ Preaching at Cookham
Regatta* and *Resurrection in Cookham Churchyard*. In his resurrection paintings he wasn't trying to depict life after death
but this world – the world of ordinary human relationships –
renewed by love. In the latter painting people climb out of their
graves to wonder and to embrace one another.

Many of the people in Spencer's paintings look strange,
even grotesque. A series entitled *The Beatitudes of Love* shows
tiny, ugly men staring adoringly into the eyes of fat, flashily
dressed women. Yet these figures bring to my mind a short
poem by John Betjeman about two lovers in a Bath tea-shop:

She such an ordinary little woman,
He such a thumping crook,

16

But both for a moment little lower than angels
In the tea-shop's inglenook.

Spencer was showing the power of love to embrace and affirm what might otherwise seem disfigured, even repellant. Certainly, love was the motive in all his paintings. He believed that it was love and not simply artistic talent that enabled him to depict the true identity of what he saw before him.

He did, I'm afraid, make a disastrous, painful mess of his own love-life, divorcing his first wife, then spending the rest of his life realizing that she was his true love, writing endless letters to her until she died. It was in 1938, whilst in the midst of this desolation, that he painted a remarkable series of studies entitled *Christ in the Wilderness*. Christ is shown as a rotund, bearded workman in the desert bending over daisies, looking at a hen, sitting with foxes and so on. Spencer wrote of these paintings that 'In Christ, God again beholds his creation, and this time as a mysterious occasion to associate himself with it.'

Perhaps the most remarkable of these pictures is *The Scorpion*. Christ is depicted sitting barefoot on the sand, gazing at a scorpion in his cupped hands, held out much as they might be to receive communion. In the face of Christ, there is a sense of the mystery of creation combined with an unutterable gentleness and compassion. It is as though, through his own pain, Spencer has been able to enter more deeply into the anguish of God. That look on Christ's face is an expression of God's pained tenderness for the whole of his creation, scorpion and scorpions of humanity alike.

THE GOD OF THINGS AS THEY ARE

7 June 1991

THE ROYAL ACADEMY SUMMER EXHIBITION OPENS TO THE public this coming Sunday. I had the privilege of preaching at the service for artists in connection with this, and then afterwards the enjoyment of talking to some of the distinguished exhibitors. At lunch I sat next to one artist with a most interesting story to tell. Although he had done some art before and during World War II, he had been very uncertain about whether or not he should make a career of it. Then one day in London, after being 'demobbed' from the army, he literally bumped into and knocked over a Polish officer. They got talking and became friends, and it turned out that this officer came to really believe in and encourage the artist's talent. So he began a long period of serious training. He somehow knew that he was meant not only to paint himself but also to teach others to paint.

Although he is now in his eighties, every day he has breakfast at 4.30 a.m., does his chores and shopping, has an early lunch and then devotes the afternoon to his pupils. Bringing out and developing their talents is what his whole life is geared up for. It is, he believes, what he was made for, and he believes that the chance encounter with the Polish officer who encouraged him was not a chance encounter at all.

He asked me whether I painted. 'I've no such talent,' I replied, 'but I wish I had.' Whereupon, of course, he tried to convince me that I did have some talent and that everyone has, if it can only be brought out.

Well, I am not sure that everyone has the ability to draw or paint decently, but I do believe that we all have a creative side to us, which we can express in different ways – not just in the so-called 'arts' but also in gardening, DIY, cooking, knitting, conversation and so on. To be human is to be creative – the Bible teaches us that, and so does Karl Marx! Indeed, Marx's main criticism of routine factory work was that it killed off this side of human nature. For work, as well as leisure, should bring out unexpected talents and so enable us to share in the creativity of God.

There is a poem by Rudyard Kipling in which everyone is seen as a painter:

And no one will work for money, and no one will work for fame,
But each for the joy of the working, and each, in his separate star,
Shall draw the thing as he sees it for the God of things as they are.

To be creative does not mean to say that we have to be 'way-out' or wildly original. It means putting oneself – our truest, freshest self – into what we are doing, using the best arts and skills with which we have been endowed, whether it is painting, cooking, computing or our relationships with others. It is this which lifts our life out of the rut of boredom and pettiness; and this is a gift which, in one way or another, we have all been given.

THE TIDE THUNDERS ASHORE

11 October 1991

ACCORDING TO SOME ACCOUNTS MRS THATCHER'S OVATION at the recent Tory Party conference lasted for some 7 minutes. One newspaper, however, approached the matter more scientifically and published a league table under the heading 'Darlings of Conference'. According to this Mrs Thatcher rated 5 minutes at 10 decibels, though on another day William Waldegrave did rather well with 3 minutes at 95.5 decibels. Michael Heseltine hit 107 decibels – even more than Mrs Thatcher – but for half the time.

Clapping, like everything human, gives vent to a variety of motives. Applause can be polite or ecstatic. We can applaud sympathetically by way of encouragement to a new performer, or tumultuously and tearfully to an old trouper on his or her last appearance. Sometimes there is a very close identification between ourselves and the one we are clapping. We are in effect saying, 'You represent my views, my feelings – neglected perhaps, pushed aside perhaps, but given a voice in and through you.'

Yet at its purest clapping is, quite simply, an expression of appreciation – a recognition of what is of value. As such it is an important, indeed crucial expression of the human spirit. In the mean, begrudging attitude that is always carping and never praising something human has died.

Clapping can also convey a wonderful sense of solidarity. A person clapping on their own may be brave but they look and feel rather foolish. In this regard opera-goers appear to be great clappers. The second, third and fourth curtain calls seem to have become almost part of the ritual, part of the occasion itself. That's not my scene, but I do find the applause from a radio concert interesting. You switch on, say, at the end of a piece from Smith Square, and the applause rolls steadily out – appreciative but not overdone – not just a splurge of emotion but a shared response to something admired. And this capacity for appreciation and admiration is, I believe, basic to a religious attitude to life. Without it we cannot even begin to enter into worship, a word which is formed from the word 'worth' – 'worth-ship'. It is a recognition of that which is of value in itself. Where there is generosity of spirit, a preparedness to praise, appreciation of nature or of other people, our lives can take off into praise of God himself.

An Irish poet of the thirteenth century, thinking especially of poems of praise, wrote:

To praise man is to praise
the One who made him.

All metre and mystery
touch on the Lord at last.
The tide thunders ashore
In praise of the High King.

Or, as Psalm 47 puts it:

O clap your hands together, all ye people:
O sing unto God with the voice of melody.

Torn Umbrella
and Royal Parasol

13 October 1997

IN DELHI A FEW YEARS AGO MY WIFE AND I WERE WALKING through a back street when my eye was caught by a man sitting on the pavement selling maps. Ever since then his image has haunted my mind with a question: How on earth did he survive? It wasn't a main road, so not many people went by; the maps were of a poor quality, so few people would have bought them anyway; and the price was so low that he couldn't possibly have earned enough to live on; but somehow he survived, and with a kind of dignity.

That makes me think of India's capacity to survive. But there is also her capacity for joy. As you drive through Indian villages you see children playing on the backs of water-buffaloes in the village pond, jumping and splashing about in sheer delight.

The writer who, for me, has really captured the essence of India is Rabindranath Tagore, a friend of Gandhi who won the Nobel Prize for Literature in 1913. One of his poems is called 'Flute-Music'. It's about a desperately poor government clerk living in a single room in a smelly alley. Even his umbrella has holes in it. Then one evening he hears someone down the alley playing some songs. Tagore writes that as the music starts,

...the whole sky rings
with pangs of separation.
At once the alley is a lie,
False and vile as the ravings of a drunkard,
And I feel that nothing distinguishes Haripada the clerk
From the Emperor Akbar.
Torn umbrella and royal parasol merge,
Rise on the sad music of a flute
towards one heaven.

The music transforms the poverty, gives the clerk a sense that he is one with any king in his yearning for love and for heaven.

Those who have studied poverty around the world say that it is even worse being poor in America than it is in India. For in America the poor are failures in a highly competitive society – they are the left-behinds, the rejects. In India, a land suffused with spirituality, the poor have a place that is not without dignity.

Torn umbrella and royal parasol merge,
Rise on the sad music of a flute
Towards one heaven.

And, as Tagore continues:

The music is true.[1]

---

[1] 'Flute-Music' in Rabindranath Tagore, *Selected Poems*, translated by William Radice (Penguin, 1985), p. 96.

WHAT KIND OF GOD?

THE TENDER MOTHER

9 July 1998

JOHNNY SPEIGHT, THE CREATOR OF THE CHARACTER ALF
Garnett, died this week. Alf was a man who was never ashamed to
mouth the most appalling opinions. But his view of God had a point:

Where's your working-class God, then? Eh? You've got your upper-
class God – oh yes. Just look at his name – *Lord* God. Not Fred God
or Harry God.

Uncharacteristically for Alf Garnett, this is in fact something of
an understatement. For according to *The Book of Common
Prayer*, God is not just any old lord. He is 'King of Kings, Lord
of Lords, the only ruler of princes'. Alf Garnett might very well
wonder whether we frail human beings have a place at all before
such a mighty monarch. And we might well wonder whether
that kind of language, which fitted in so well with the absolute
monarchy of the sixteenth century, has any resonance with us
today. Even Mrs Garnett might wonder, in her forthright way, if
the men weren't having too good a thing of it. Not only is the
language monarchical and hierarchical, it is male.

In Alice Walker's novel *The Color Purple*, Celie says:

Man corrupt everything ... he tried to make you think he everywhere. Soon as you think he everywhere, you think he God, but he ain't. Whenever you trying to pray, and man plop himself on the other end of it, tell him to git lost.

So for a fair number of people today religious language is rejected on moral grounds; or more usually it has simply gone quite dead on them. The situation is a serious one; far more serious than many in the churches care to acknowledge.

The question is whether there are resources in the Christian tradition to revitalize our picture of the divine in a way that resonates with us today.

A verse I like comes from the prophet Isaiah:

Look to the rock from which you were hewn,
to the quarry from which you were dug.

The mystery in whom our being rises is a rock – and the record of this in the Bible is a quarry in which we may still dig for fresh images and life-giving metaphors. There's no need to think of the Holy One as a sixteenth-century despot in the sky.

The Church of England is presently busy revising its liturgy with a view to a new prayer book in the year 2000. A phrase in one suggested new prayer goes:

How wonderful the work of your hands, O Lord.
As a mother tenderly gathers her children
you embraced a people as your own.

I can hear Alf Garnett snorting. But even he might acknowledge that there is something here that he can respond to.

GOD'S SPIES

25 February 1994

'RICK' AMES, THE TOP CIA MAN WHO WAS CHARGED WITH spying for the Russians, was alleged to have done it for money. I don't underestimate the power of money, but there are usually also other reasons why people become spies – sinister ones like blackmail, or ideological ones, as with Burgess and MacLean and the other Cambridge students who were recruited to the Communist cause in the 1930s. Perhaps, too, there is in some people a psychological propensity to become a spy. In the story of his early years, *A Sort of Life*, Graham Greene related how uneasy he felt when he was a pupil at the school where his father was the headmaster. It made him feel like a double agent – a spy for his father in school and a spy for his friends at home. It was this, he thought, which gave him a lifelong interest in the themes of loyalty and betrayal.

Yet I wonder whether even such psychological reasons go deep enough, or are adequate to explain the fascination which spy stories hold for so many people. We are all, at least sometimes, conscious of dual loyalties, with a loyalty to our family and friends and so the society in which we live on the one hand, and another, higher, haunting loyalty to we know not quite what on the other. Jesus called this other loyalty the kingdom of God, in contrast to the kingdoms of this world. When the Bishop of Edinburgh came to conduct a mission in Oxford a few years ago, he gave it the title 'Another King, Another Country'. Not everyone is able to be so definite as to say there is another king, another country; yet there is something in the idea which evokes a response at a level deeper than the psychological. Immersed in this world as we are, we sometimes sense that we truly belong elsewhere, and that we can betray not just people or a country but something else altogether, to which we are ultimately accountable.

In Shakespeare's *King Lear* the sad King tells Cordelia that they had better go to prison together, where they can spend their time talking about everything under the sun. 'Let us,' he says, 'Take upon us the mystery of things/As if we were God's spies.' Together they would explore the mystery of life and death, as though they had secret knowledge of the meaning of existence. Though locked in prison, they would see things from a privileged inner vantage-point.

Of course, there is irony in Shakespeare's words. We can never fully fathom the meaning of what's going on, the mystery of human existence. We can't be God's spies. Yet irony depends for its force upon a positive relation to the truth. We do belong elsewhere as well as here. We do have dual loyalties. Somewhere inside us we carry secret truths that help us to make sense of life and to live it rightly.

A DIVINITY THAT SHAPES
OUR ENDS

23 July 1993

A FRIEND ONCE TOLD ME ABOUT THE THREE GREAT LIES
that run through modern life. The first is, 'Darling, I'm sorry,
I'm working late at the office.' The second goes, 'Don't worry
about it. There's a cheque in the post.' And the third runs,
'Good morning. I'm from Head Office and I'm here to help
you.' We distrust Head Office – whether it's the BBC, Brussels
or the Church Commissioners. For example, there exists a deep
suspicion of Brussels bureaucrats; and no doubt they do their
fair share of moaning about our failure to fall in line with their
tidy schemes.

In the New Testament Jesus refused to adjudicate in political conflicts of this kind. Instead he called on everyone to
repent – and by that he did not mean stirring up vague but use-
less feelings of guilt. The Greek word that he used – *metanoia* –
means re-thinking our lives, changing our outlook, in the light
of God's presence with us. For those at headquarters, like bishops, it means seeing how much we tend to impose our own
paper plans on others without taking their views into account.
For those on the edge of an organization it means being aware

of our tendency to scapegoat the centre, to blame them for problems which are of our own making. For we often project on to others, including God, our own faults or limitations, which are inherent in life itself.

A fine film called *The Fencing Master* (directed by Pedro Olea, 1992) tells the story of an upright, just man who is totally absorbed in the carefully controlled, artistic world of fencing. But outside, in the streets of Spain in 1868, there is nothing but the uncontrolled violence of riots. At one point he muses, 'God tolerates the intolerable. God is no gentleman.' The fencing master thought he had his own private world perfectly organized, whilst outside, the divine plan – if there was one – seemed to have broken down completely. We sometimes do feel that all is chaos.

Yet, as Shakespeare put it, 'There's a divinity that shapes our ends, rough-hew them how we will.' There is a divine purpose, but it is of the essence of that purpose that we have been given freedom to discover it and to co-operate with it; but often we chop it about and shape it very roughly indeed. God is not a Brussels bureaucrat, and it's no good blaming the headquarters of the universe, because HQ has chosen to work through the infinite variety and richness of human choice. It's up to us – and down to us, for that matter.

Do Not Presume

4 May 1998

A BOOK ABOUT MARY BELL, A CHILD MURDERER, WHO HAD herself been terribly abused as a child, will be published tomorrow. Sadly, the debate about this and the controversy over released paedophiles seem to totally lack any Christian dimension. But the Christian view of existence has truths that are crucial to these issues.

First is the fact that there is a darkness in all of us; one that we are very reluctant to acknowledge. When things go wrong, whether at home or nationally, our instinct is to blame other people. So, in the Genesis story, Adam blamed Eve and Eve blamed the snake. Worse than this, we project our unacknowledged fears on to others. So we get scapegoats and witch-hunts and the whole hue and cry of the popular press. For example, it is, of course, vital to take the greatest possible care in discharging convicted paedophiles into the community. But to demonize them, as has happened, ignores the fact that most child abuse is perpetrated by someone already known to the victim.

Then we ourselves are never in a position to make a final judgement about whether a person could or could not have acted differently. We have to make provisional judgements about who is at fault – the whole criminal justice system depends upon it – but the full truth is another matter. Mary Bell was herself terribly abused as a child. And about someone else who has been vilified it has been said: 'In the lost childhood of Judas, Jesus was betrayed.' Only God knows the pressures people are under. Only God knows whether I have done better or worse in my circumstances than Mary Bell or Judas Iscariot in theirs.

Then, hard though it is to take in, the Christian faith asserts that there is no one who is beyond the scope of Christ's redemption. He came to save all who will be saved. On the cross, one of the criminals turned to Jesus and said, 'Lord, remember me when you come into your kingdom.' Jesus replied, 'Today you will be with me in paradise.'

This scene haunts Samuel Beckett's play, *Waiting for Godot*. An important part of the background of this play for Beckett was some words of St Augustine: 'Do not despair; one of the thieves was saved. Do not presume; one of the thieves was damned.'

Demonizing a person or particular group of people is always deeply unhealthy. The Christian faith bids us instead to look at the seeds of evil in ourselves and put our trust in the one who came to save us. Criminals need to hear Augustine's words, 'Do not despair.' Some of us, perhaps, are in no less need of hearing his other words, 'Do not presume.'

SPIRITUAL POWER

26 October 1994

A NUMBER OF JURORS IN A MURDER TRIAL USED A OUIJA board to reach a verdict, and as a result, it was reported yesterday, a retrial will be necessary. This is one example of the way that superstition is taking hold in our society, but it's not the most startling. A book called *The Celestine Prophecy* has just been published here after racing to the top of the American best-seller lists with sales of more than 1.5 million. Its theme is that the universe is made up of an invisible spiritual energy that is open to human manipulation. The book says that we can perceive this energy glowing luminously around other people and that, amongst other things, those who increase their spiritual energy will become invisible and travel straight to heaven. Apparently books in this genre now account for 20 per cent of sales.

Yet some of this seems like an uncanny echo of more mainstream beliefs. After all, I believe in a universal, invisible energy – I call it the Holy Spirit; and the Bible also records spiritually dynamic people, like Elijah, disappearing straight into heaven. The difference, however, is focused in the word 'manipulation'.

The assumption behind the use of ouija boards and other occult activities is that by saying or doing certain things you can manipulate this energy to your advantage. At the heart of Judaism, Christianity and Islam, as well as some other religions, however, is the insight that we live before the Holy One – to whom we are accountable and whom we cannot manipulate.

And that brings out the other difference between the mainstream faiths and these age-old occult beliefs that are now so much in vogue: we can have them on our own terms, with a nice warm glow, a frission of excitement – and that's it. But Jesus said, 'Anyone who would be a follower of mine must deny himself, take up his cross and follow me.' Christianity is about discipleship – a day-by-day surrender of the clamant ego to Christ and others.

Edmund Burke claimed that superstition is the religion of weak minds. It might be more accurate to call it the religion of weak wills.

And I wonder about Halloween. All Saints Day is one of the great Christian festivals, when we celebrate the presence with us of the hallowed ones – those who are for ever luminous with Christ. But this has nothing to do with ghoulies or ghosties, let alone trick or treats. So I'm glad that the Mothers' Union, which does excellent pioneering work, now produces a pack for an alternative Halloween party, which has already shown itself to be great fun for children. Such things are needed. For as G. K. Chesterton put it, when people stop believing in God they don't believe in nothing – they believe in anything.

STRENGTH IN WEAKNESS

9 December 1994

IT MUST BE EXTRAORDINARY TO BE PRIME MINISTER OR A Cabinet Minister at the moment – to come down to breakfast and be confronted by the morning's newspapers – the scorn, the howls, the baying for blood. I imagine it evokes a curious mixture of reality and pain. Yet, political turmoil, however tough, hardly affects us as deeply as private griefs and sorrows. Of course, public issues have far-reaching consequences, affecting great numbers of people for good and ill, but the disarray of a government does not carry the anguish of a disintegrating marriage. An adverse vote in the Commons cannot compare to the loss of a child. Many felt a real pang when they heard that Gordon Wilson, the forgiving father who lost his daughter in an IRA bomb explosion, has now lost his son also in a car crash. So when events conspire against us, if we are yet able to rely on family and friends we have what matters most – personal support and, when appropriate, good advice.

On this programme yesterday the former Prime Minister Jim Callaghan was asked what advice he would offer John Major. The advice I thought of – of a strictly non-political kind applicable to all of us at difficult times – was memorably put by Rudyard Kipling in his poem 'If':

If you can keep your head when all about you
Are losing theirs and blaming it on you,
If you can trust yourself when all men doubt you,
But make allowance for their doubting too...

And so on, through four verses, to the final refrain which says that if we can do all that, we will indeed be a man. All good, stern Victorian stuff – yet perhaps too strong for many of us. I once said cheerily, to someone who had come to see me, 'It's a great life if you don't weaken.' 'Yes,' he said poignantly, 'but I *do* weaken.' And so do we all from time to time – we feel that life is just too much. Which is why Kipling's advice, brave as it is, won't do in the end. It's fine if we are feeling moderately on top of things, but it's not if we are not – then it only makes us feel even more inadequate. At those times I prefer the words of St Paul. He had some debilitating weakness – no one knows quite what it was. He wrote: 'Three times I besought the Lord about this, that it should leave me; but he said to me, "My grace is sufficient for you, for my power is made perfect in weakness."' And he went on to say, 'For when I am weak, then I am strong.'

When things are going badly for us, the way through is not to rely on our own strength – we are none of us moral supermen – but to make friends with our weakness, our temptation to give up, to crack under pressure. That way we can discover the power beyond our own power.

THE IMAGE REMAINS

8 February 1991

AS I WAS GOING THROUGH LONDON YESTERDAY I PASSED BY cordoned-off Whitehall, and I felt suddenly aware of the vulnerability of all human institutions. And yet, thank God, the essentially democratic and ordered fabric of our society remains strong. This is in sharp contrast, for example, to the Soviet Union, from which I have recently returned. As someone there put it to me, 'It's like living in a fairy story. The deeper you get into it, the more frightening it becomes.'

Yet, despite the anxieties and the day-by-day difficulties of life in the Soviet Union, for the Church there this is a time of remarkable growth. Literally thousands of formerly closed churches are being opened up again. I happened to go into one in a village in Estonia. There the old priest, complete with a white beard and a twinkle in his eye, was only too glad to talk to my friends and I, even though he had been taking services all day. Building materials lay on the frozen ground outside, wooden scaffolding reached up to the ceiling and some superb murals were being painted on the walls. The old man told us that he lived on 30 roubles per month (about £3 at our rate of exchange) and the food that the villagers brought him. We are all called to serve God, he said, but he had been set in this particular place to see his church rise again from a state of dereliction.

Restoring church buildings is a wonderfully specific task. More testing is the new educational and social role that the churches in the Soviet Union must now play. The churches are able, indeed encouraged, to form bands of social workers to minister in or even to run hospitals. As recently as 1988 the head of the Soviet Government's Department of Religious Affairs asked critically, 'Is it right, in this great socialist society of ours, to allow a man's dying vision to be a Christian bringing him a bedpan?' The answer now is 'Yes', and the Moscow Baptist Church, for example, has organized groups of people to tend and counsel psychiatric patients in a hospital that only recently held dissidents. The churches have not only survived the long years of persecution. They are a continuing witness to the triumph of the human spirit over evil.

One of the places we visited was Kronstadt, the old naval port of St Petersberg (still for the moment known as Leningrad), where before the Revolution there had lived a spiritually magnetic priest called John, who is now regarded as a saint. There the church, which from 1923 had been a factory, was being restored, and worshippers were coming into the chapel for evening prayer. John of Kronstadt once wrote:

Do not confuse man, the image of God, with the wickedness that is in him, for the wickedness is only accidental, his misfortune, a sickness, an illusion of the devil; but his being, the image of God, still remains.

Conscious as we are today of terrorism and war, and the wretched cruelty of the world, I am grateful for the conviction that, despite everything, in all of us the image of God still remains.

TRANSFIGURING LOVE

1 February 1991

LAST WEEKEND I WAS IN THE SOVIET UNION TRYING TO foster some practical co-operation between the Russian Orthodox Church and the Church of England. We stayed in the countryside at a lovely convent dedicated to prayer and work (mostly farm labour done by hand). The scene was calculated to arouse all our most romantic notions: row after row of bare birches rising out of the snow; the green onion-shaped domes on the church rising into the wide sky; and the nuns in their mysterious black hats moving silently in the northern light.

Some evocative photographs hung on the convent's walls, and one in particular caught the eye: a row of Sisters, in their habits, swinging scythes as they cut the grass for hay. As we gazed one Sister remarked firmly, 'And very hard work it is too, from five in the morning until ten at night.' If we had any further illusions about the nature of their life they were quickly dispelled when we saw the Sisters looking after their cattle at their farm, where the soil is frozen for half the year. Realism broke in upon our romanticizing – which was a good thing, for romanticism by itself is simply escapism.

Our sense of enchantment was at its highest during the church services. The haunting Orthodox music was sung by two choirs, while candles flickered amid the icons and the reverent worshippers. At one service I could not help noticing a rather restless mentally handicapped boy being looked after by his mother. They were there again for the Sunday morning Liturgy. The child, now calm, arms devoutly crossed, came up to receive communion, held by his mother. In a flash I seemed to see the whole life of that mother: the disbelief and pain when she first discovered that the child was handicapped, the disappointments, all the difficulties and struggles. Yet above all I saw that mother's love: her arms, firmly but gently round her son, guiding him to communion.

The convent was in Estonia, so we were highly conscious of the trauma in the Baltic Republics. Whenever I could I listened to news from the Gulf on the World Service. Yet this peasant mother and her child reminded me that world events, on however vast a scale, come down in the end to particular individuals who suffer and struggle. That mother revealed something else also: the transforming power of human care. The truth in human romanticizing is the possibility of things being different, better, more beautiful. And this is real, not just escapism, for it is a true insight into the transfiguring possibilities of love, which is capable of turning the ordinary into the wondrous, human anguish into the material of eternity.

Cosmic Optimism

14 August 1992

SOMEONE TOLD ME THIS WEEK THAT ONE MORE ILLUSION
had gone. They had been brought up in the shadow of World
War II and had come to believe that war in Europe was a thing
of the past and that, however gradually, the world was becom-
ing a better place. It is difficult to believe that today, with war
raging in Bosnia. My friend felt that his optimistic assumption
had been pulled from under him, leaving him somewhat confused about where God is in all this.

The Christian faith ought, I think, to dispel our illusions –
not just about other people but about ourselves too. Whatever
ideals I may have, whatever hopes I may have about myself, I
can never be sure how I would behave under pressure in different circumstances. The same destructive tendencies that we see in
Bosnia are also present in me; in me there is a seed of the same
cruelty. We can sincerely thank God for our long-established
political institutions which check the worst excesses of violence
in our society, but we share the same nature with all other
human beings.

The Christian faith opens our eyes to ourselves and to the world as it is. But it also keeps us from despair and from the cynicism that is close to despair. In even the most terrible situations there are people who are trying to act differently. I was heartened to hear of those Serb villagers who have been protecting Muslim refugees from their fellow Serbs. I have been encouraged by the Serbian Orthodox Church's critical stance towards their own government. If there are no depths to which we cannot sink, there are also glorious heights of human heroism to which some people rise. In truth there are no 'nice' people. We are all potential devils and potential gods.

So there is no automatic progress towards a better world. That great religious philosopher, Woody Allen, once posed the question, 'What makes God laugh?' Well, what *does* make God laugh? 'Tell him your plans for the future,' was Woody Allen's answer. Yet equally, there is no inevitable slide into the kind of horrors that we are hearing about daily. We have the capacity to bring good out of evil, to take constructive action in the midst of destructiveness.

The novelist William Golding once described himself as 'a universal pessimist but a cosmic optimist'. That gets the Christian perspective about right. There is nothing that cannot go wrong; there is no safe plateau. But there is always a good that can be done, and that good will not be wasted. For me, as a Christian, that hope is rooted in the death and resurrection of Christ, who entered our darkness and, for the sake of us all, rose to new and eternal life. In union with that life Christians seek to bring something good out of the present mess. But for us all, because our last illusion has gone, the challenge is to do the best of things in the worst of times.

WHAT IS MOST WORTHY
OF LOVE?

9 June 1995

WHEN I GOT INTO A TAXI EARLIER THIS WEEK THE DRIVER spotted my clerical attire and immediately asked if I was going to join in the protests against the showing of Martin Scorsese's film *The Last Temptation of Christ* on television. (It's a rather poor, vulgar production, in my opinion.)

But whilst I was still groping for an answer the driver told me that he and his fellow Muslims had been writing scores of letters of protest against the film. It was wrong, he said, that a holy man like Christ should be portrayed in that way.

I felt in a rather odd position. Here was I, a believer in Jesus as the Son of God, a Christian Bishop to boot, apparently doing nothing to stop a scandalous portrayal of Christ, whilst my Muslim friends were mounting a campaign.

I believe in freedom of speech, and I accept that those on the cutting edge of art have to take risks, especially in the depiction of religious themes. I value living in a society where people can criticize and mock sacred cows. For such a society, whatever its faults, is less bad than one in which a particular ideology is imposed. But that conversation with the Muslim taxi driver does raise one fundamental question: Is anything sacred in our society now? After all the knocking and mocking, what, I wonder, are we prepared to value – really value? A person whom I much admire, Austin Farrer, once put it this way:

What is the supreme motive of a truth-seeking mind? Is it to explode shams, or to acknowledge realities? ... After all the detection of shams ... a man must make up his mind what there is most worthy of love, and most binding on conduct, in the world of real existence.

Actually, I'm not totally pessimistic about our society. Yesterday it was reported that a gynaecologist had been struck off the medical register for falsifying his research. What is noteworthy is the rarity of such cheating and the bedrock assumption in the scientific community that the accuracy and honesty of research really matters.

The exposure of lies and evasions, the mocking of hypocrisy and pomposity – all this is vital. But it assumes a desire to get at the truth of things: and going the whole way means discovering that reality – that personal reality – in whom all truth is grounded, and who is most worthy of love.

THE CHRISTIAN WAY

STILLNESS

15 August 1995

NOISE IS ONE OF THE GREAT MENACES OF MODERN LIFE. SO many people will be grateful for the new legislation that is being finalized this week. There will be on-the-spot fines for noisy neighbours of £40 rising to £1,000. And there are a lot of noisy neighbours about – more than 300 complaints are received per day, and a recent poll revealed that 1 in 10 households now consider that their life is ruined by noise.

All this will no doubt please the devil in C. S. Lewis's *Screwtape Letters*, who boasted that he would make the whole universe a noise in the end. 'Noise,' he said, 'which alone defends us from silly qualms, despairing scruples and impossible desires.' That's why, although we hate noise, we are also rather frightened of silence. Silence can bring to the surface all kinds of uncomfortable thoughts which we would rather not have to face. Yet silence is essential because those thoughts do have to be worked through, and then that silence leads into stillness – stillness of the mind's racing and the heart's restlessness, which points to what T. S. Eliot called 'The still point of the turning world'.

But how to find that silence? Some love to go on country walks near Oxford, but so many roads have judderingly loud surfaces that traffic roar fills the air for miles around. Indoors can be no better. In West London, where I used to live, we calculated that school classes lost 20 minutes a day as a result of aircraft flying overhead. In a short story by Heinrich Böll the main character goes to extreme lengths to get quiet. He works in a recording studio. Whenever he has to cut a tape because a speaker pauses for a moment he doesn't throw it away. He collects all these silences, splices them together and then, when he is at home in the evening, plays back the tape to himself. He even gets his girlfriend to sit in silence whilst he records it. 'Oh Rina,' he says, 'If only you knew how precious your silence is to me. In the evening, when I'm tired, when I'm sitting here alone, I play back your silence.'

That's only fiction – but some people are feeling that desperate. The physical and psychological effects of noise are now well documented. We all need some peace and quiet for our sanity; and from a religious point of view, silence prepares the way for stillness. 'Be still and know that I am God', says a verse in one of the Psalms. And I love the answering response in another Psalm: 'Truly, my soul waiteth still upon thee.'

Doing it Thy Way

18 May 1998

IN 1968 FRANK SINATRA PICKED UP WHAT WAS ORIGINALLY A French song and recorded 'My Way'. And the rest, as they say, is history. 'I did it my way' has become one of the best-known lines of our time, even sung at funerals.

I don't propose simply to mock it. When anything gains such a degree of popularity there's often some nub of truth nudging to get out. The truth here is that each one of us *is* unique. There never has been and never will be – even with cloning – someone just like you or just like me. And, quite rightly, we want our life to be *my* way – not just a following of the crowd or a copy of anyone else. The point was well made by an ancient sage, Rabbi Zusya, when he said: 'In the coming world they will not ask me: "Why were you not Moses?" They will ask me: "Why were you not Zusya?" '

That's the nugget of truth in wanting to do it my way. But we do not discover our unique self simply by striving to be different; still less by rejecting the moral norms which are the breath of life to any human society; and even less by cutting ourselves off from the source from which our being flows.

In 'My Way', the singer prides himself on being 'not one who kneels', but our capacity to recognize what is of worth and to offer worth-ship, or worship, is an essential part of being human. The desperate attempt to be different leads to isolation and conformity. There is a terrible sameness about the selfish and cruel. By contrast, the saints – for example, Paul, Augustine and Francis – are all gloriously different. In putting themselves fully at the disposal of the divine way, they have become rich themselves. Each one of us is very special. We have a perspective on existence that no one else will ever share. We can bring gifts to God that no one else can ever bring. We have work to do which is ours alone. Evelyn Waugh, commenting on a character in one of his novels, wrote: 'God wants a different thing from each one of us, laborious or easy, conspicuous or quite private, but something which only we can do and for which we were created.'

That's why I prefer the motto 'I'll do it thy way', following the example of Jesus, who prayed, 'Not my will but thine be done', and who taught us to say, 'Thy will be done on earth as it is in heaven.'

BEYOND FEAR

8 August 1995

THERE WAS AN INTERVIEW IN YESTERDAY'S *TIMES* WITH Mandi Norwood, the new editor of *Cosmopolitan*. But this woman, who has brought explicit sex to women's magazines, revealed that she was scared every day of her life. 'I can never fully enjoy what I do,' she said, 'because there's always this element of ... *fear*.' When pressed she said it was the fear of 'being found out', of being a poor, ordinary girl who once sat in her room in Newcastle.

Hardly much to be afraid of, when people are being pounded by guns in the former Yugoslavia, and when we see civilians with terror-stricken faces fleeing their homes, heading for an unknown future. Yet fear is fear – however surprising the form it takes. I was talking recently to two distinguished barristers, and one said that the only reason why he would give up his job was fear. He admitted to a fear of drying up, of his mind going blank in the middle of a case. One of my great heroes is Dr Johnson. His friend Mrs Thrale wrote about what she called 'A secret far dearer to him than his life', and in a footnote referring to their friendship added, 'A dreadful and little suspected reason for *ours* God knows – but the fetters and padlocks will tell posterity the truth.' So great was Johnson's fear of insanity that he gave Mrs Thrale a padlock, with strict instructions that if he ever snapped she must fetter him and lock him up in a private room.

Fear of one kind or another runs all through life and is part of all of us. The Bible works on this assumption, and Jesus was quite direct about it. Luke's Gospel, for example, records these words:

I tell you, my friends, do not fear those who kill the body, and after that have no more they can do. But I will warn you whom to fear: fear him who, after he has killed, has power to cast into hell; yes, I tell you, fear him.

It makes me want to close my Bible and move away fast. But the very next verse continues:

Are not five sparrows sold for two pennies? And not one of them is forgotten before God. Why, even the hairs of your head are all numbered. Fear not; you are of more value than many sparrows.

Jesus accepts that fear is part of life. He says, in effect, that if we are motivated by fear, we should fear what is truly to be feared. But if we focus there, we will paradoxically discover how greatly we are valued. Fear not, he said, the very hairs of our head are numbered. Difficult to believe – very difficult – but that's what he said.

Our Nobility –
and Its Obligations

11 October 1995

I ENJOYED THE TRIBUTES TO LORD HOME YESTERDAY. THE lady who ran the local wool shop summed it up for many when she said simply, 'He was a true gentleman.' Another local remarked, 'He had dignity, decency and integrity.' This judgement was echoed by politicians. Edward Heath, for example, remarked that 'He was completely trusted by everyone.'

Clearly Lord Home was a decent man and a fine Christian. But it would be false to idealize that generation of politicians in order to contrast them with today's, allegedly all on the make. Patrician politicians had ambitions too.

Then, if one has been brought up on a lovely estate by a loving family, it ought to be possible to be decent. If you can't develop a good character with that sort of start in life, where does that leave the rest of us?

The great strength of that kind of background was, of course, its tradition of public service. Apparently Lord Home's mother once remarked, 'I think it's so good of Alec to do Prime Minister.' Being Prime Minister was a chore you took on out of a sense of duty. *Noblesse oblige* – noble birth imposes obligations.

But this principle is not just applicable to the aristocracy. It is firmly rooted in the New Testament – from those to whom much is given, much will be expected. The parable of the talents recognizes that life does deal people very different hands – some have only one talent, others ten. The question is how we use what we have been given. And Jesus makes it quite clear that we are ultimately accountable.

The concept of *noblesse oblige* sounds old-fashioned today. The whole idea of noble birth seems out of place. Yet, rather than discarding the notion altogether, I would like to see it expanded, extending to embrace the whole of humanity. 'What a piece of work is a man', mused Hamlet:

How noble in reason! How infinite in faculty!
In form, in moving, how express and admirable!
In action how like an angel!
In apprehension how like a god!

There is indeed a *noblesse* that we all share; for we are made in the image of God. You can't get more *noblesse* than that, even if you can trace your ancestry back 30 generations. And that *noblesse* does *oblige* – does carry obligations.

SOBER DETERMINATION

3 June 1994

THE RELATIONSHIP BETWEEN CHRISTIANITY AND WAR HAS always been a complex, uneasy one. Sometimes in the past the Church has undoubtedly been far too militaristic. But there was little glorifying of battle 50 years ago as a million Allied soldiers waited to land in Normandy. In the tense, waiting days, the poet Keith Douglas, who was killed after the landings, wrote a poem which began:

Actors waiting in the wings of Europe
We already watch the lights on the stage
And listen to the colossal overture begin.
For us entering at the height of the din
It will be hard to hear our thoughts,
Hard to gauge
How much our conduct owes to fear or fury.

Like others, he was conscious of his mixed feelings and was apprehensive about how he would conduct himself in battle, whether in fear or fury.

Another person to whose mind we have access at this time was a young officer called Hugh Dormer, who, sadly, was also killed shortly afterwards. At the end of May he wrote in his diary:

We were inspected on the sea front by General Eisenhower ... God grant me the courage not to let the Guardsmen down, knowing as I do how they count on me, I ask only that he do with my life as he wills.

A little later the diary reads:

I face the adventure in sober determination, knowing how I shall feel and knowing that modern armoured warfare is hell, and complete hell, and nothing else, with no nobility or fineness about it, but only humiliating fear. Once again at Mass this morning in the village church I offered my life to God to do with it entirely as he chooses.

That phrase 'sober determination' does, I think, get the mood right. For those like him, who were Christian, there was also that profound sense of their life offered to God. It is an attitude which goes back to Jesus himself in the Garden of Gethsemane, when he prayed that he might not have to drink the cup of suffering, yet still he managed to pray, 'Nevertheless, not my will but thine be done.'

That sober determination, that sense of duty, underpinned for many by a strong desire to do God's will, has gone deep into our culture. We see it in our soldiers serving in Northern Ireland and with the United Nations in Bosnia, amongst the police as they face increasing violence and amongst countless people as we take up the daily tasks that have to be done. In many ways we are a very different society now from 50 years ago – but I do not believe that sense of duty has completely gone. And it is every bit as necessary for building a better society today as it was on those Normandy beaches.

NO PORKIES

29 January 1998

THERE'S A POWERFUL MOMENT IN THE TV SERIES *A TOUCH of Frost* when David Jason's eyes bulge and he focuses on someone with the words, 'Mr Jones, I think you're telling a porky.' Whatever the ultimate truth of the Clinton saga, a lot of 'porkies' have already been told.

What I miss in all the allegations and the discussion about whether they will bring Bill Clinton down is any strong sense of disapproval of lying *per se*. When David Jason's eyes widen, and he says in that deep voice with a slight rasp in it, 'I think you're telling a porky', there is the unmistakable note of hostility – of moral disapproval.

Lying, at any time, under any circumstances, is a serious matter, for it destroys the very basis of our relationship with one another. It's quite right that the Ten Commandments – the basic rules which any society needs in order to hold together – should have as number nine, 'Thou shalt not bear false witness against thy neighbour.' But common-sense reflection on life leads to the same conclusion. Relationships with one another are only possible on the presupposition that for most of the time we can be trusted to mean more or less what we say. Of course, people do sometimes lie: but without an underlying assumption that the truth is being told, no human relationship would be possible – and in the end there would be no human beings, for the development of human personality is inescapably social. In short, to define oneself as a human being is, logically, to commit oneself to telling the truth.

Of course, there are so-called 'white lies' when, for example, out of kindness, we avoid actually telling someone they are ugly. There is even, in the interests of the State, what politicians today like to call 'economy with the *actualité*'. But these blurred edges should not disguise the fact that deliberately to lie is not only to distort our humanity; it is to destroy it.

There is a terrible statement in the Gospels where Jesus is reported as saying that every sin can be forgiven except the sin against the Holy Spirit. I take this to refer to a deliberate refusal to recognize what you know in your heart to be true. It can't be forgiven because if we continue to reject what we know to be truth, we make ourselves into people incapable of receiving any truth.

But that's rather a depressing note on which to end. There are some hopeful words in relation to this theme from a rather surprising source, the French novelist Emile Zola. He wrote, 'Let all be made known that all may be healed.' In the end, all will be made known and, pray God, all will be healed.

SELF-DISCIPLINE

6 March 1992

THE GREAT DR JOHNSON WAS ONCE ASKED WHETHER HE would like a little wine. 'Certainly not,' he replied. 'I would like a lot of wine or none at all.' He was a man of extremes. After he had given up alcohol permanently, he could still drink 25 cups of tea in an evening. And there are many others, I suspect, who are all-or-nothing people, who find moderation difficult.

I've been surprised recently to discover a number of people who have adopted a personal discipline over alcohol. Sitting next to a celebrity at dinner, I noticed that he didn't have any wine. He told me that he had a personal rule to abstain for the first week in every month. Another person who took me out to lunch called the wine waiter to see what I would like and then told me that he went without alcohol every other month. That's all very laudable, I'm sure, but personally I welcome the structure provided by the Church – the rhythm of fast and feast, Advent followed by Christmas, Lent followed by Easter. Given the excesses of so much of our consumer society, frankly it is a blessed relief to come to a time in the year when as Christians we are expected and encouraged to live simply with self-discipline and to enter more deeply into the mystery of Christ.

The Scriptures are, however, adamant about one point. In the Book of Isaiah, for example, these words are attributed to God:

The kind of fasting I want is this: Remove the chains of oppression and the yoke of injustice, and let the oppressed go free. Share your food with the hungry and open your homes to the homeless poor (Isaiah 58:6).

In short, if you have to choose between a life that is self-disciplined but selfish and one that is dedicated to human need though blighted by excessive smoking or drinking, choose the latter. You will die younger but you will have helped other people. These are, however, false alternatives. The whole point about true self-discipline is that it releases energy for others by bringing us up against the great realities of life – first of all, God. For a Christian, as indeed for a Jew, a Sikh or a Muslim, the fundamental fact of existence is our utter dependence on a source beyond ourselves, not only for our food but for all that we are. And this increased awareness makes us more conscious of human need and the obligation to do something about it. Every day through the post I receive letters and circulars from wonderful organizations desperate for more money or more help. One way of ensuring that our personal discipline over food or drink serves a positive purpose is to link it with a definite resolve to do something extra for others – for our favourite cause, perhaps, or a neglected area of human need.

Lent is a good time. It can bring us back to the big, important things. And it gives us an enhanced sense of life itself, a greater joy in the simple, taken-for-granted details.

LEARN TO WAIT BEFORE GIVING ALL YOUR LOVE

26 March 1993

I HAVE BEEN VISITING A GOOD NUMBER OF SCHOOLS recently, and in one of them, as I was being shown around, it was suggested that I shouldn't go into a particular class, as they were in the middle of a sex education lesson. I was glad they were having such a lesson; and I was glad that they were taking it seriously enough not to want visitors barging in.

This week it was revealed that 8,000 girls under 16 become pregnant every year – an average of 2 for every secondary school in the country. Good sex education, at an early enough stage, is obviously a crucial element in lowering this figure. And all of us would agree that good sex education means not just biological details of the facts of life but also helping children to think about relationships and the meaning of love.

Within all of us there is a desire to give ourselves fully to and receive fully from another human being. From a Christian perspective, in which we are a unity of body, mind and spirit, the giving of ourselves physically is meant to be an expression of commitment – not just for the intensity of the moment but over a period of time, and through all the ups and downs of life.

Of course, when it comes to sexual matters, we are all failures – but there is still an ideal. As the psychiatrist Jack Dominion puts it:

Once a person has involved the whole of our being, it is natural to wish to continue that relationship, and commitment means continuity, reliability, predictability and responsibility for each other.

And this, on a Christian view, reflects the faithfulness of God's love for us.

Because of the large number of pregnancies amongst school-age girls, there has been a call this week for free contraceptives to be issued to all teenagers. But there is a better way: good sex education, and the re-establishment of an ideal of what it is to enter into a truly committed relationship.

In 1943 a woman called Rose Scholsinger was executed for her resistance to Hitler. Knowing that she was going to die, she wrote to her young daughter in the following words:

Do not be too prodigal of your feelings. There are not many men who are like your father, as good and pure in their love. Learn to wait before giving all your love – thus you will be spared the feeling of having been cheated. But a man who loves you so much that he will share all suffering and all difficulties with you, and for whom you can do the same – such a man you may love, and believe me, the happiness you will find with him will repay you for the waiting.

That is a voice from another age, but it still has a place today. As a teacher in a large comprehensive told me yesterday, it is not only a mistake but an insult to underestimate the innate sense of decency and dignity that is still there amongst young people.

MUTUAL RESPECT

22 October 1993

THIS WEEK'S TRIAL AND ACQUITTAL OF A UNIVERSITY OF London student for 'date rape' makes the theme of *Oleanna*, a play now showing in London, even more relevant. The play focuses on the relationship between a student and her teacher. The student is somewhat nervous, not to say neurotic, and in the first act her teacher is being encouraging and pastoral. Then, in the second act, we discover that the student has brought charges of sexual abuse against him. These charges are totally false. But he is reported and, as a result, he seems likely to lose his job. It's a play which fiercely divides the audience. I suspect that the majority feel very much on the side of the man who is being falsely accused. Yet because it is a good play the ending is much more open than that. Certainly, I was left with some real sympathy for the position of the girl.

The play is particularly powerful in the way it depicts, symbolically, the power relationship between the man and the woman. It begins with the girl huddled into herself on a hard-backed chair whilst her teacher sits above her on the desk, being paternalistic. Then the roles are reversed. He sits withdrawn whilst the girl, with a new-found confidence, struts about the room berating him. Yet although the girl student was technically wrong, you are able to enter into her state of mind, in which she felt dominated by males in a world in which males still have most of the power.

This is, of course, now beginning to change. Indeed, some men are beginning to feel redundant. A series of interviews on a housing estate recently amongst single mothers brought out very clearly the fact that irresponsible, immature men were now simply being jettisoned, and the women were organizing their lives with their children in their own way.

The New Testament simply assumes a world in which men are powerful and women are meant to be submissive. But there is nothing sacrosanct about the cultural world in which the Gospel was first preached. It has begun to change and needs to change further. What we take from the New Testament is not the social order but the change in the spirit and the quality of the relationship between women and men that it sought to bring about. In the Letter to the Ephesians the writer says that a wife must be subject to her husband, but it goes on to say, 'Husbands, love your wives, as Christ also loved the Church and gave himself up for it.'

It is, I believe, important to try to achieve equality. If a dwarf meets a giant on the road, however kind the giant is, the dwarf is always likely to feel intimidated. But a balance of power by itself is not enough. An inner transformation has to take place. It is that inner transformation with which the New Testament is concerned. Whether we move into a world in which women are totally dominant, as men have been in the past, or whether, as I hope, there will be a genuine and appropriate equality, the mutual respect, affection and affirmation which we all desire will still depend upon what goes on in our minds and hearts.

THE HUMAN TENDER REVERENCE

4 December 1992

YESTERDAY THE QUEEN CAME TO OXFORD, FIRST OF ALL to celebrate the four hundred and fiftieth anniversary of the Diocese of Oxford – a very happy occasion – and then to fulfil some other public engagements. Like other people, I have great admiration for the Queen, for the dignified and conscientious way in which she fulfils her many duties. But there was a time when I was a truculent republican. When I was an adolescent the national anthem used to be played at the end of every performance in a cinema or theatre. I can remember fierce rows with my mother when I refused to stand up. In recent years the whole nation seems to have gone through that rebellious mood, with all our ancient institutions being attacked.

One of the greatest changes that has taken place in the last 30 years has been the decline in deference. Until the late 1950s European civilization had been built of the principle of hierarchy. At the top there was God, then there was the monarch by divine right, then there were the aristocracy and the Church. You deferred to those above you and exacted obedience from those below you. It was assumed that without all this, civilization would simply collapse. 'Take but degree away,' wrote Shakespeare, 'untune that string and hark what discord follows.'

Well, there may be much discord in our society – including, sadly, bombs such as the one that exploded in Manchester yesterday – but it has not collapsed. And the benefits of open debate, including fierce criticism, are too many to be given up. Yet we need something to hold us together, and something other than permanent, negative hostility.

The Christian faith has never really been as wedded to hierarchy as previous generations thought it was. The heart of my faith is a God who came amongst us as a vulnerable human being, who did not impose his will but who wins my allegiance. As a phrase in one of the Eucharistic Prayers puts it, 'He opened wide his arms for us on the cross.' He opens his arms to *embrace* us, opens them wide to embrace *all* of us, opens them on the *cross*, where he soaks up our hostility. And this, I believe, changes our whole perception of other people.

In one of his poems D. H. Lawrence is fiercely scathing of all forms of subservience. Yet he continues with the words, 'but when I see the life spirit fluttering and struggling in a man I want to show always the human tender reverence.'

When I see people struggling on through great difficulties, trying to cope with courage and dignity despite everything, then, whoever they are, I would like to be able to show that human tender reverence.

ETERNAL SOULS IN THE MAKING

5 February 1996

THERE'S A LOVELY ITALIAN FILM BEING SHOWN AT THE moment called *Il Postino* or *The Postman*. It's about a slightly simple young man who gets to know a well-known poet. The poet even helps him learn to write poetry so that he can woo the girl he's in love with. At one point in the film the naive postman clearly feels mystified and very hurt by the poet's behaviour. But he buries the pain deep inside him and still tries to think well of his famous friend. Like others in the audience, I was caught off guard and found it difficult to restrain a tear for his attempts to put on a brave face.

These days we are all encouraged to show our emotions – to grieve and to weep. But I can't help thinking of all those millions of people, like that young man, who sternly hold their sorrow in check and somehow steel themselves to go on. The poet R. S. Thomas makes the point when he refers to some of his parishioners with the words, 'Their hearts, fuller than mine of gulped tears'.

Over the weekend the television news showed pictures of the appalling devastation in Bosnia in those areas which are now in the process of being handed over as a result of the peace deal. Whole villages and towns have been devastated, with every single flat and house gutted, on the horrific basis of 'If we are not going to have it, neither are you!' There will be terrible grief in the days ahead as people begin to go back and see what has happened to their homes. Yet people *will* go back, and somehow they will begin to rebuild their lives.

The ability of human beings to go on despite everything, in the most adverse circumstances, always seems to me a witness to something mysterious. I don't think it can be accounted for simply in terms of an animal will to survive. This comes across powerfully in D. H. Lawrence's novel *Sons and Lovers* when Paul Morel visits his sick mother. She worries that his life is all struggle and battle. She wants him to be happy. 'No,' he replies, 'so long as you don't feel life's a paltry and miserable business, the rest doesn't matter, happiness or unhappiness ... Say rather you want me to live.' By 'live' he does not mean 'live it up' but living with courage and integrity.

Here, as in so many lives, there is an underlying sense that the meaning of life is not found in balancing pain and pleasure. Rather, the struggle to go on itself matters. In our efforts to cope, to rebuild life after whatever disaster, we indicate that something hugely important is at stake: to put it in old-fashioned language, eternal souls are in the making.

WHAT KIND OF SOCIETY?

THE BUSINESS OF BUSINESS

15 May 1992

ONE OF THE MANY FAILURES OF THE CHRISTIAN CHURCH IS our neglect of the world of work. The majority of people spend eight or more hours a day, five or more days a week, for forty or more years trying to earn a living. But if you went to the average church service you would never suspect it. Even worse is the way we have, in recent years, appeared to be anti-business. Yet industry and commerce is what, in one way or another, we all depend on. So it was good that this week the Archbishop of Canterbury, in his characteristically forthright fashion, raised the question of the purpose of business. Its purpose, he said, is 'to serve people by creating things of use and value to them'.

Some wanted to dismiss this as airy-fairy idealism remote from the real world – but for 20 years this is precisely what the best American business schools have taught, and this is what an encouragingly large number of companies now believe. For example, the constitution of one large American group states:

The business of business is serving society, not just making money. Profit is our reward for serving society well. Profit is the means and measure of our service – not an end in itself.

That, I think, gets it about right. Another way in which business is moving away from the old stereotype of 'anything for a profit' is by the adoption of company mission statements with a strong ethical content. Some of our most profitable companies are also those with the most wide-ranging ethical codes. Instead of letting the shareholder reign supreme, they have developed what is called 'the stakeholder approach'. This assumes that there are a number of groups who have a stake in the company – people who have claims and rights. Employees, customers, suppliers and the wider community are all stakeholders in this sense.

The market economy reflects certain important Christian values, like free choice and personal responsibility, but it also has negative features. Like all human institutions, including the Church, it expresses the will to power, greed and human aggrandizement. Those of us who live and operate in a market economy always need to be on the alert for the way that it can harm those who are least able to stand up for themselves, not only in this country but in the developing world. Nevertheless, this is the system we have, and this is the context in which many devout Christians are set. One of the great rediscoveries at the time of the Reformation was the idea of the lay vocation. From this point of view it is as Christian to be a banker as a bishop, as godly to be a shop assistant as a nun. For Christ is Lord not only of churches and monasteries but also of the markets and exchanges of the world. The pressures and conflicts of business do not make this easy, but it is an exciting and creative context in which to serve.

BUT FOR THE GRACE OF GOD

4 February 1994

TWO MEN WERE COMPARING THE EXTENT OF CORRUPTION in their countries. 'The difference between us,' said one, 'is that you can still recognize corruption. We simply take it for granted.' And that, I suppose, is the good news hidden in the allegations against the police in Stoke Newington. We still have the capacity to be shocked. We may have terrible failures, but the standards are still there. And it is desperately important that we keep those standards of public probity; that government servants should do their jobs without backhanders; that the police should apply the law impartially.

This week the Lord Mayor of London addressed the Archbishops and Bishops of the Church of England. He assured us that the City was fundamentally an honest place – that financial scandals were rare. May that indeed be true of the City, the police and every department of our public life. But with creeping corruption in so many countries of the world today, extra vigilance is needed.

Even with that vigilance, however, some will get away with it. We heard yesterday not only about the police but about the collapse of charges of war crimes against 17 people now living in Scotland. We were told that there was not enough evidence to bring criminal proceedings. That may be so. But there will be a final judgement when no crime will go undetected. This could sound like very bad news – the Church just trying to scare people, as in the old days. But, on the contrary, it is good news. For it means that the universe, despite all appearances, is built on a foundation of justice. In the end all will be revealed. Those who have done wrong will be brought face to face with the harm they have done to others.

Yet we can't totally distance criminals from ourselves. As the police know, in uncovering crime they have to enter deeply into the criminal mind. This is not a comfortable thing to do. The best thriller writers suggest that there can sometimes develop a strange, symbiotic relationship between a detective and a criminal. And this makes me wonder about the whole British fascination with crime. Hundreds of new crime stories are published every year. You can't turn on the television without seeing yet another police series. At the least it shows the extent to which we share the same human nature.

So whilst in no way blurring the distinction between those who act out their impulses and those who don't, I cannot forget what John Bradford said in the sixteenth century when he saw some criminals being led away to execution: 'But for the grace of God, there goes John Bradford.' This is true. 'But for the grace of God, there goes Richard Harries.' For if there is an affinity between us and even the worst criminal, it must indeed be by the grace of God that I live – grace which includes forgiveness, acceptance and new life in Christ.

The Sacrament of Taxes

5 October 1994

'TO TAX AND TO PLEASE, NO MORE THAN TO LOVE AND TO be wise, is not given to men.' Words of Edmund Burke which seems to be hanging heavily over all politicians at the moment. At Blackpool the Labour Party is desperate to convince the electorate that its policies won't cost the average taxpayer more, whilst the Tories are still trying to persuade people that they are the party of low taxation. I wish they wouldn't be so anxious to please. Taxes are a good thing and paying them is a spiritual matter.

Of course, no one wants waste. Taxpayers' money must be used in the most effective way possible. But that said, taxes are one of the signs that we belong together in a society that seeks to be civilized. First, of course, quite a lot of tax goes to pay for what we actually get. We are all beneficiaries of the police, schools, and transport system and hospitals. Then, quite properly, some of our taxes go to support those in need. In our best moments we all want to ensure that, for example, the frail elderly are looked after in their declining years, or that families with a sick child get all the medical ancillary help that is available.

Taxes ensure that what we would want for ourselves, or for others when we really think about it, happens as a matter of course and is not dependent on passing generous impulses. And taxes are a sign that as a society we want such things to happen. We don't want care to depend solely on the good will of a few. We want it to be a feature of the whole community.

One of the marks of the Church in the New Testament is the way it looked after the poor. Paul, for example, went to a great deal of trouble to raise money from the churches round the Mediterranean for those in need – and he saw this as a fundamental sign of Christian fellowship, an essential mark of what it meant to belong to one another in Christ. That, of course, was voluntary. But the motive behind taxes need not be totally different. They too are a sign of our solidarity with one another and a mark that we wish as a society to have certain decencies, certain standards of care, for everyone.

And the point about taxes is that we do not have to rely on whim for this. Taxes can go some way to ensuring that what we want for those whom we know personally in our more enlightened moments takes place even for those we do not know, even in our less enlightened ones. Taxes are a good thing, a sign – perhaps we could say a sacrament – that we belong together within the one society. If politicians of any party ever have the courage to say this, I hope we could surprise them by the strength of our support.

MORE AND MORE OF WHAT?

22 May 1992

A FAVOURITE VERSE FROM ONE OF MY FAVOURITE POETS, Gerard Manley Hopkins, goes like this:

What would the world be, once bereft
Of wet and of wildness? Let them be left,
O let them be left, wildness and wet;
Long live the weeds and the wilderness yet.

Not surprisingly, this is a verse which the Green Movement has taken to heart. Like so many people in the South-East of England, I have a nightmare in which our beautiful countryside is covered with tarmac and concrete, and the air is polluted by fumes and the noise of cars and planes. For all of us, nature is a source of renewal, and this isn't just paganism. The spirit of 'freshness that lives deep down things', as Hopkins put it, is the Holy Spirit, who touches and quickens our souls.

And yet there is a terrible dilemma. People need houses and, in the developing world, they need a growing economy in which all can share. The Earth Summit which will soon meet in Brazil somehow must hold together the need to save the planet for the future and the need to save people from starvation now.

My wife ensures that our household follows a Green code. I stamp empty beer cans flat and pile them in a box. We collect bottles and paper for recycling. But I did baulk the other day when I read an article entitled '24 hours in the life of a good Green'. After telling me to save water, it then urged me not to buy imported fruit and vegetables because their transportation uses up fuel and so pollutes the atmosphere. Here I have to admit a bias. I enjoy the variety of fruit and vegetables available in our shops. But more important, what about a developing country whose only source of foreign currency is, say, the banana crop? Poor countries need to trade in order to buy the technology to develop.

A businessman friend of mine, Kenneth Adams, argues that it is the essential nature of human beings to want more and more. But now, here in the developed world, we should be channelling this desire away from material goods into education, music, culture, recreation – and God, in whom this desire is rooted, for he wishes to give us more and more of himself. We cannot, nor should we want, to get rid of the idea of growth. But we need to look for growth in those areas which do not pollute the environment and which do not use up non-renewable resources. It is false to think that we can do without growth, which is a God-given sign of life.

The desperate need in the developing world is for appropriate and sustainable material growth, enabling the one billion people in the world who are living at or below starvation level to enjoy something of the life that we take for granted and which God wills for all his children. The overwhelming need in our society is for growth in the quality of life. The two kinds of growth are linked. For the more we go for growth in the quality of life in our own society, the less we will ruin the environment and the more we will care about those for whom economic growth is, literally, a matter of life and death.

LOOK TO YOUR HEALTH

21 February 1992

THE SEVENTEENTH-CENTURY ANGLICAN WRITER ISAAK Walton was a keen fisherman. Perhaps it was those long hours standing by the slow stream which gave him his sense of perspective on life. Anyway, he once wrote:

Look to your health; if you have it, praise God and value it next to a good conscience; for health is the second blessing that we mortals are capable of.

Few, I imagine, would want to disagree with that. We know how easy it is for even the tiniest pain to fill the mind, whilst a major illness clouds all that we do. What Walton called 'the second blessing' matters – to all of us.

Yesterday the Labour Party published its manifesto on the Health Service. There are important arguments to be heard about GP budget holding, Hospital Trusts and so on. But given the fact that there will never be unlimited resources, there are, however, no specifically Christian insights to decide between the policies put forward by Labour or the Liberal Democrats or the Conservatives on how those resources are best organized, provided that we accept the foundational principle of a civilized society: the best possible health-care available for everyone, whatever their income.

A baby born into a family where both parents are unemployed has a need for exemplary medical care. The mother has as much right as the wife of a millionaire to the best ante-natal and post-natal treatment. If, sadly, the babe is diagnosed as suffering from Downs Syndrome, the expensive and continuing specialist help that will be needed is something that we as a country are pledged to provide. All this, I take it, is basic to our society and has been since 1945. Let us argue keenly about the means without losing sight of the end – the maximum chance of health for everyone.

It has been fashionable in recent years to knock Britain, but one of our glories has been the health-care available to all our citizens. Whether we can still take the same pride now is something that people differ about, but I am quite sure that we ought to be able to take pride in this – even more than in the biggest battleship or the smartest regiment.

There is a fine passage in a little-known book of the Bible, Ecclesiasticus, which affirms, first, that all healing comes from the Most High, and then goes on to say:

The Lord created medicines from the earth,
By them he heals and takes away pain ...
He gave skill to men
That he might be glorified in his marvellous works.

God works for our wellbeing. Although we often have to suffer sickness and disease, these are contrary to his will. But he has given us the resources and the skills – medical, human, political and administrative – to heal and care.

Health was Walton's second blessing. His first was a good conscience. As a society we need always to test whether we can have a good conscience about the standard of health provision available to everyone.

LIFE IN THE WOMB

27 October 1997

I SPOKE RECENTLY TO A HOSPITAL CHAPLAIN WHO IS ON the front line of support for mothers who have lost babies during pregnancy. As part of her care she offers parents a short service before the foetus is cremated. Some of those present will have had their pregnancy terminated because of severe foetal abnormality. It's not difficult to imagine their grief, guilt and confusion. And sometimes a person can be haunted for years by the thought of a baby they chose not to have.

On this difficult subject I remind myself that it is the mother who is pregnant; it is she who will have to agree to an abortion if, tragically, that proves to be necessary; it is she who will give birth if the pregnancy goes ahead; and probably it is she who will bear most of the responsibility for the child's upbringing. So her feeling and wishes are to be fully taken into account. But, that said, the teaching of the Church of England, as expressed in successive resolutions of General Synod, is that abortions should be rare and exceptional. A statement of the Board for Social Responsibility says that because the foetus has the right to live and develop as a member of the human family,

We see abortion ... as a great moral evil. We do not believe that the right to life, admits of no exceptions whatever; but the right of the innocent to life admits surely of few exceptions indeed.

The teaching of the Roman Catholic Church is quite clear – abortion is wrong under all circumstances, even when the life of the mother is at risk. In the light of this, it is easy to caricature the teaching of the Church of England as liberal or woolly. But it isn't. We share with our sister church a strong opposition to abortion, differing only in holding that there can be a few, strictly limited, conditions under which it may be morally preferable to any available alternative. Perhaps this is what the framers of the 1967 Abortion Act had in mind. But whatever they meant, something has gone gravely wrong. There are now over 170,000 legal abortions every year; and in some places the Act is interpreted so liberally that in practice there is abortion on request.

We cannot simply change the Act overnight. As Cardinal Hume said yesterday, first we have to change hearts and minds. There is a long haul ahead: the whole moral climate must change so that the unborn child is taken into account as fully as the mother. For as a 1983 resolution of the Church of England's Synod put it:

All human life, including life developing in the womb, is created by God in his own image and is, therefore, to be nurtured, supported and protected.

THE COMMUNITY AT REST

16 July 1993

'REMEMBER THE SABBATH DAY, TO KEEP IT HOLY. SIX DAYS you shall labour and do all your work; but the seventh day is a sabbath to the Lord your God.' The quotation of a commandment like that today is hardly likely to get a hearing, let alone wide assent. Instead it arouses the questioning, sceptical part of our minds. Someone has given me a cartoon showing Moses on a mountain, with the tablets of the Law in his hand. Moses says, 'And man shalt be in charge and have all the best jobs ... and woman shalt dust and obey.' Beside him is a group of tough-looking housewives, one of whom shouts out, 'He's making it up!'

We could say just the same about the sabbath law – it's not God telling us, but Moses or the people of Israel making it up. I believe, however, that in this commandment to keep one day of the week special for God and one another, there is not only wisdom but divine wisdom. God puts this before us for our wellbeing – for our spiritual, psychological and physical health. 'Getting and spending we lay waste our powers', wrote Wordsworth. We need a day to recuperate and recover a sense of what life is really about.

This week the Government published four options on Sunday trading, with total deregulation – simply letting market forces rip – at one extreme. Some change in the law is necessary, but the special quality of Sunday needs to be preserved – not just for the convenience of church life but for the health of the nation as a whole. Too easily we accept the idea that religion is a purely private matter, with the rest of life being governed by economic factors. A small but revealing incident in the life of a Catholic journalist brought the point home to me. He drove into a filling station for petrol, where he saw a Muslim take out his prayer mat and devoutly say his prayers facing Mecca. He said it made him regret, for the first time since the 1960s, that he had given up saying grace in public in restaurants. It was not just in the 1960s that we began to tuck religion away inside ourselves – the process goes back many centuries. Yet religion is very much concerned with the way society as a whole lives and with the values that underlie all our public institutions – it is all under God. The fact that we have prayers in Parliament and a sovereign who is crowned in church is an acknowledgement that there is a higher authority to whom politicians and all of us are accountable.

The Bible sets before us the ideal of a whole community resting – spending a day together simply enjoying God and one another. This could now seem like an idealistic notion. But it still remains, I believe, what our good Creator wants for us – because it makes for our wellbeing.

THE POLITICS OF FORGIVENESS

10 June 1994

ON 10 MAY I PAID MY FIRST VISIT TO THE SOUTH AFRICAN
Embassy. With others, I had been invited to celebrate Nelson
Mandela's inauguration as President. Suddenly, on the big
screen in front of us, the ceremony came through live from
South Africa. As we raised our glasses and fists and sang and
cheered, it was difficult to stop the tears trickling down one's
cheeks. It seemed, literally, miraculous. And although appalling
news is now coming from Rwanda, where vast numbers of
people have been murdered, hopeful news continues to come
from South Africa. There is to be an amnesty for politically
motivated crimes committed under apartheid. Those who con-
fess to the official commission will be spared punishment.

And yet this will hardly be good news to the many who
have suffered. Staying with us at the moment is an old friend
from South Africa, who is now a Bishop. As a young man he
was one of those who were imprisoned on Robben Island for
opposing apartheid. He told me that in prison he said to himself that when he was released he would spend his first two
years of freedom as an ordinary policeman getting his own

back. He does not feel like that now, but his own experience gives him a real feeling for those young people who have seen their friends and parents murdered or maimed. People can talk too easily of forgiving and forgetting. The apartheid regime was truly terrible, with countless cruelties to its name; it was responsible for state-sponsored terrorism not only in South Africa itself but also in the surrounding countries. All this will have to be brought out into the open. As the Minister of Justice has said, 'Disclosure of the truth and its acknowledgement are essential.'

I would want to add that, if there is to be real forgiveness, as opposed to a political amnesty, it can only be offered by those who have suffered. We cannot offer forgiveness on behalf of other people. Furthermore, forgiveness is never cheap. For the Christian, the cross of Christ is a measure not only of God's love for us but also of the cost of forgiveness, the hurt that is held in the heart of God.

Yet what is being attempted in South Africa now – what we might call the politics of forgiveness – is a genuinely creative move, a sign of something very special happening. For in a world where we are all flawed, where there is no perfect society just round the corner, the only way we can hold together and go on together is through a mutual acceptance rooted in God's acceptance of us – which is why Jesus taught us to pray, 'Father, forgive us our sins, as we forgive those who sin against us.' The amnesty in South Africa could be more than a piece of prudence. It could be a way of making that prayer a political reality.

SELF-APPOINTED AGITATORS

30 October 1992

AS I WAS COMING BACK FROM LONDON IN THE TRAIN EARLIER this week the scene in the carriage was much as usual – a few people immersed in their papers, the rest of us half dozing after a long day. Suddenly we were jerked awake by a man standing in the gangway delivering a speech. 'Oh dear.' I thought. 'Is this going to be some embarrassing religious harangue?' But the man – a well-dressed, well-spoken regular commuter – concentrated on the faults of that particular railway line. He pointed out to us that in the last week there had been a 70 per cent failure rate on the evening commuter train. He urged us to act – at least to sign a petition that he was getting up. At the end, far from being embarrassed, we applauded warmly as he went on to the next carriage to deliver the same message. I particularly liked it when he said of himself, 'I don't represent any organization. The only authority I have is that of a self-appointed agitator.'

And I thought of other 'self-appointed agitators' – what they have achieved and how so many of them have ended up. In particular I wondered about that figure who disturbed the

IN THE GLADNESS OF TODAY

routine of everyday life round the Lake of Galilee all those years ago. 'Self-appointed agitator' is certainly how some saw him. For what distinguished him from other teachers of the time was that he wants us to live as if the future is already here. He made that ideal world, which lives in the imagination of us all, present. He invited us to enter now into the Kingdom of God's love. The question that his message raised then hangs over him still, and will continue to do so until the end of human history: Was he a self-appointed agitator – or a God-appointed one?

Agitators can be embarrassing, awkward people, but when they have a sense of humour, as the man in the railway carriage did, and as I believe Jesus did, they really do wake us up out of our dozy routine and get us to question our complacent acceptance of things as they are. And how much we need such people today, with the general air of collapse all around. Another rise in crime figures reported this week, the breakdown of the ambulance computer system, the erosion of moral standards...

So great is our sense of collapse that, absurdly, we blame the Government for everything. The Government has real responsibilities which they and only they can carry out, but to reverse this collapse, to raise standards in every area of our life, from getting the trains to run on time to feeling safe and being able to trust other people and their word again, we need some more agitators – preferably ones with humour and a sense of the presence of God's rule today.

TRUE PEACE

14 October 1993

WHEN MARTIN LUTHER KING WAS IN PRISON BECAUSE OF HIS campaign for civil rights a group of 20 pastors wrote to tell him to cool it, to stop being a troublemaker. He replied, 'Peace is not the absence of tension but the presence of justice.' That's a very biblical view. The wonderful Hebrew word *shalom* means the whole world flourishing, everyone finding their proper fulfilment. Those who work for that vision, who disturb an unjust status quo, can seem to be awkward or difficult people – which is presumably what was meant by the reported words of Jesus, 'I came not to bring peace but a sword.' I wonder if the Nobel Peace Prize Committee, who announce their winner today, will go for that kind of troublemaker.

Or perhaps they will select a reconciler. The Northern Ireland women who won the prize a few years ago remind us of those thousands of good people there who have prayed and struggled for reconciliation over the years – moving across barriers, outside the tribal boundaries, rejecting stereotypes – and often, as a result, bringing the wrath of both sides down on them. Anyone who has ever tried to reconcile two squabbling members of a family or two estranged friends knows that you are not always thanked for your efforts. In the teaching of Jesus such reconcilers have a special place of honour. 'Blessed are the peacemakers,' he said, 'for theirs is the kingdom of heaven.'

There's another kind of peace that I suspect the Nobel Prize Committee will not be considering – the serenity that we sometimes see in our friends and hanker after for ourselves. It's not political enough or high-profile enough for a prize. Yet inner disharmony expresses itself in outside enmity; and this in turn creates or reinforces the divisions among us. Peace is indivisible, and at its centre is the deep, inner quiet that comes from a union of our lives with God. 'Peace I leave with you,' says the Christ of John's Gospel. 'My peace I give unto you. Not as the world gives, give I unto you.'

'Peace' is a precious word; it is that for which all human beings long. But it is also a word that is easy to distort or corrupt. It's been used to put a pious gloss on oppression, to avoid facing conflict, to have our ease at the price of other people's misfortunes. There are many kinds of peace that we must reject. So, even apart from the political pressure on the Nobel Committee, recognizing the right kind of peace is a major task. That's why I like this prayer that is often used by the Corrymeela Community, who work for reconciliation in Northern Ireland.

Show us, good Lord
the peace we should seek,
the peace we must give,
the peace we can keep,
the peace we must forgo,
and the peace you have given
in Jesus Christ.

It's a prayer that recognizes that searching for true peace is a human and spiritual struggle.

REDEEMING THE WORLD

TOGETHER IN YOUR HEART

25 October 1991

I WAS FIRST IN JERUSALEM NEARLY 30 YEARS AGO, AS A student. I stayed in the compound of the Anglican Cathedral – a little piece of England abroad, complete with a neat garden full of roses. It was a lovely, peaceful place. And yet just around the corner was no-man's-land, where the buildings were scarred with bullets and everywhere there were reminders of the wars that had been fought in 1948 and 1956. Since then there have been four more wars in that part of the world, involving countless acts of cruelty, terrorism and brutality.

The suffering and the tears cry to heaven, 'How long, O Lord, how long?' So if I could be granted just one miracle, it would be for a successful outcome to the talks that begin in Madrid next week. If we believe the gloomy predictions of the political commentators, a miracle will indeed be needed. To be more precise, I am praying for a miracle for the moderates.

People sometimes think of moderates as soft or cynical, manipulating the middle ground that has been created for them by the bravery of the extremists. But moderates in this situation have their own brand of courage. When Lord Jacobovits, the

Chief Rabbi in England, made some mild remarks about the need for Israel to be sensitive to Palestinian suffering, the bitterness of the criticism that he received from some quarters both surprised and shocked me. Moderate Palestinians are in an even worse situation. Sometimes they end up paying with their lives for their willingness to negotiate.

A few days ago an Israeli, a Palestinian businessman from the West Bank and a Jewish rabbi came to talk to me about a new organization with some fresh ideas. They are bringing together Palestinians and Israelis in small groups to talk about contentious issues like the use of water from the Sea of Galilee and the security fears of both sides. And this is just one of a number of little-publicized groups that are trying to break the stereotypes and are working for a true reconciliation. There are rabbis in Israel who march for peace, and there are communities in which Israelis and Arabs live and work together.

Moderation means recognizing the suffering, the fear and the aspirations of the enemy and taking them fully into account. We all have a role to play in this. There is a prayer written by a Palestinian Christian which says:

Pray not for Arab or Jew,
For Palestinian or Israeli,
But pray for yourselves
That you may not divide them in your prayers,
But keep them both together in your heart.

For it is by keeping them together in our hearts that violence begins to be moderated, and from there springs a new future which includes the other. Please God, a miracle for the moderates: it may be our last hope for a long time.

GODLY AND QUIETLY GOVERNED

8 October 1993

EARLIER IN THE YEAR I WENT WITH THE ARCHBISHOP OF
Canterbury on an official visit to Georgia. We were fortunate
to have a long session with the President, Eduard Shevardnaze
– to whom we all owe so much for his crucial role in ending the
Cold War. He was having a bad time then, with two civil wars
going on, a precarious political base and virtually no control of
the army. Now things seem pretty desperate: he has lost a chunk
of the country to his rival, and the papers yesterday were full of
pictures of Georgian refugees fleeing along icy mountain paths.

For me those old prayers from *The Book of Common
Prayer* for a stable political order have taken on new meaning –
prayers that we may be 'godly and quietly governed'. Since the
Second World War people have been driven, quite properly, by
the desire for independence and greater social justice. Now, not
only in Georgia and Russia but in Somalia, South Africa, the
Sudan and Bosnia and so many other places, the crying need is
for stable government, for order as well as justice.

Towards the end of our time with Mr Shevardnaze the
Patriarch of the Georgian Church, who was also with us,

presented the President with an icon of St George and some candles, assuring him of our continuing prayers. This was not just a polite gesture. A year before this Shevardnaze had become an avowed Christian, taking the name of George. The gift was to celebrate the anniversary of his baptism.

I was assured that the President's new-found faith was perfectly sincere – yet there is no doubt that it is also valuable for political purposes. The same is true in Russia. Although Boris Yeltsin is not, so far as we know, a believer, he has made a point of making friends with the Church and being seen at the Liturgy. In the recent crisis he called in the aid of the Church as a mediator. The countries of the former Soviet Union know that they need an alternative ideology to Communism to hold them together, and their leaders believe that religion can help to unify and motivate people. The first Christians unashamedly prayed for this. As the First Letter to Timothy puts it, 'I urge that prayers be offered for sovereigns and all in high office, that we may live a tranquil and quiet life.'

The prayers for civil order that run through the Prayer Book are deeply felt, for they come from the sixteenth and seventeenth centuries, when our own country was racked by civil war. It is a measure of the relative stability of our own political system that, with the possible exception of Northern Ireland, such prayers have not seemed so urgent. When I was younger the collect asking God that 'this world may be so peaceably ordered by thy governance that thy Church may joyfully serve thee in all godly quietness' struck me as rather unheroic. Surely, I used to think, we need more than that. Yet that peaceful ordering, enabling us to live in 'godly quietness', is just what so many people in the world are now desperate for.

MAY GOD HAVE MERCY
ON ALL OF US

5 February 1998

THERE WERE TERRIBLE SCENES OUTSIDE THE JAIL WHERE Karla Faya Tucker was executed in the early hours of yesterday morning. A Gospel singer's 'Amazing Grace' was shouted down by cries of 'Kill the bitch!' The song witnessing to the fact that Karla Tucker had converted to Christianity was drowned out by shouts reminding us that she had done something terrible, for which she deserved to suffer.

In the film *Decalogue* by the great Polish director Kieslowski, there is one story based on the commandment, 'Thou shalt not kill.' A youth murders a taxi driver in a most brutal and apparently motiveless way. The youth is caught and we see him hanged. As the noose went round his neck and the body dropped I was filled with a great sense of sadness, but also struck by the pointlessness of his death and how it demeaned the society that insisted on it. I feel the same about Karla Tucker's execution. However deserved it may have been – and it was – it was also demeaning.

Karla Tucker herself, as someone who was deeply sorry for what she had done and had turned to Christ, is in good company. When the criminal beside Christ on the cross said, 'Lord, remember me when you come into your Kingdom', Jesus replied, 'Today thou shalt be with me in Paradise.' And in Christian art that criminal has traditionally been shown as the first person through the gates of Heaven, greeting other people as they come in.

Yet it is possible to speak too glibly of forgiveness. We can sympathize with Mr Thornton, whose wife was so brutally pick-axed to death by Karla Tucker, when he said, 'My religion says to forgive. I'm not a perfect man, I've tried pretty hard. I still can't do it.' Indeed, there is a strong *moral* case against forgiveness, as Ivan protests in Dostoevsky's great novel *The Brothers Karamazov*. Yet, however important it is to keep the victims in mind and not cheapen their suffering, I see no other basis for society except the one that Jesus gave in the Lord's Prayer: 'Father, forgive us our sins, as we forgive those who sin against us.' So my sympathy finally lies not with Mr Thornton but with Karla Tucker's brother, who cried out, 'Karla was totally rehabilitated by the prison system. And what did they do? They executed her. May God have mercy on all of us.'

THE HEALING OF MEMORIES

18 October 1995

IT'S GOOD TO LEARN THAT AFTER THE STALEMATE THERE
are signs of movement in the peace process in Northern
Ireland. Yet, it's not surprising that progress is slow. After all,
England has been connected with Ireland for more than 800
years. It was only in 1922 that we handed over the South, an
event immediately followed by a civil war. It takes time for
memories to be healed and for attitudes to be changed.

This week I saw a new play called *The Steward of
Christendom*, which is a remarkable contribution towards that
healing. The author, Sebastian Barry, has based the play on his
great-grandfather, a figure whom the family preferred not to
think about. Not only did he work for the English, but he was
head of the Metropolitan Police in Dublin, and was responsible
for putting down riots. In fine writing that can stand compari-
son with Synge and O'Casey, we are drawn sympathetically
into the mind of someone who is highly politically incorrect by
today's standards – a Catholic Irishman who felt a great love
for the British Empire and who felt proud to be a servant of
Queen Victoria.

The story of Thomas Dunne is a sad one. History revealed him to be on the wrong side, regarded as a traitor by many of his fellow countrymen. He lives in a mental institution, where he has been put by one of his daughters. His wife died giving birth to their third daughter. That daughter, his favourite, fled to Canada. His young son died in the 1914–18 war. When he is in the mental home, tormented by one of the warders and confused in mind, old memories come to the surface. Yet some of these memories are suffused with a lyrical hope.

One of them is of a time in his childhood when his beloved dog killed a ewe. His father told him to get the dog, but young Tom, knowing his father would put it down, stayed out with him all night. When he did return, terrified, expecting to be punished, his father clasped him to his side in sheer relief that his son was alive; and the dog's crime was never spoken of. Tom reflects:

And I would call that the mercy of fathers, when the love that lies in them deeply like the glittering face of a well is betrayed by an emergency, and the child sees at last that he is loved, loved and needed and not to be lived without, and greatly.

And he knows not only that he is loved but that he loves his own son who was killed in the War, and his son loves him still. Somehow, it saves the sadness of his life and lifts it into a new dimension, and it transcends too the violent politics of the time.

Today is St Luke's Day. St Luke was a healer; and healing has not only to do with the body but also with the mind and memories. In Ireland today, however slowly, there is a healing of memories, both personal and communal.

THEY TOO ARE FELLOW
HUMAN BEINGS

23 June 1997

THE LETTERS P-H-I-L HAVE A SOFT, SOOTHING SOUND –
'phil'. Their origin is equally pleasing, for the Greek word
phileo means 'I love'. So we have words like 'philosophy' (love
of wisdom), 'philanthropy' (love of humanity) and so on.
Unfortunately one of these words has come to have more sinister overtones – 'paedophilia', love of children. What should be
pure and selfless has come to mean what is perverse; and more
evidence of this aberration is uncovered every week.

France, for example, is now convulsed by what is being discovered in the sleepy town of Mâcon. There, 600 suspects have
been arrested and thousands of child pornography videos have
been seized. It's also now known that every year 5,000 tourists
fly to the Third World from Germany alone to look for sex
with children under 13.

In the light of this emerging evidence it is quite right that as
a country we are thinking very hard about the most effective
way to protect children. And we are quite properly having
to do this in the churches as well. Each diocese now has to
appoint a child protection adviser, and anyone who works with

children – not only clergy but youth leaders and Sunday school teachers – will have to go through standard vetting procedures, including checking for possible criminal records. To someone like myself, brought up in the 1940s, it's almost unbelievable – but the age of innocence has passed. When the nineteenth-century clergyman Francis Kilvert travelled by train he tended to fall in love with any little girl in the same compartment. They seemed to him like angels, and he wrote about them ecstatically in his diary in a way that simply would not be possible now. There is loss in that – but now that our eyes have been opened, the wellbeing of children has to come first.

Yet at the same time, we cannot lose sight of the fact that paedophiles, even when convicted of disgusting crimes, are fellow human beings. William Golding's most ambitious and least understood novel, *Darkness Visible*, is in part about the redeeming of a paedophile – a teacher called Mr Pedigree. At the end he is caught up in his old compulsion outside a lavatory in a park where children are playing, when he has a kind of vision. A boy whom he despises, who is also a kind of saviour figure, appears to him, wading along 'waist deep in gold', as Golding puts it. Mr Pedigree understands that they are 'in a park of mutuality and closeness where the sunlight lay right on the skin'. We are led to believe that there is something better even for Mr Pedigree. Children have to be protected – that is paramount. But no one is outside the scope of divine redemption.

THE LONG RIVALRY

29 October 1993

OCCASIONALLY WE COME ACROSS SOMEONE WHO SEEMS A really good person. I knew a man like that once – a Consultant at one of our major hospitals who gave himself day and night to his sick children. Indeed, I think it was over-work that led to his tragically early death. He was always caring, patient and full of smiles. At the centre of his life was his religious faith, and although he worked so hard, he still kept Ramadan, which involves not eating during the hours of daylight. Yes, he was a Muslim – and he brought home to me, a Christian, the spiritual resources there must be in Islam to produce such a lovely person.

The Prince of Wales has just given a major lecture on Islam and the West, trying to dissolve some of our more unhelpful stereotypes. Here, I think, a sense of history helps to put things in perspective. The first English historian, the Venerable Bede, writing in the eighth century, recorded the sense of shock in Europe when a people whom he called the Saracens invaded Spain. In succeeding years they swept almost all before them until the end of the seventeenth century, when rain came to Europe's rescue. The forces of Islam were bogged down in the mud around Vienna. So for a thousand years the attitude of Europe to Islam was one of fear – fear before an apparently inexorable advance. Then, in the eighteenth century, with the gradual weakening of the Ottoman Empire, fear gave place to a mixture of disdain and fascination with what Europeans thought of as the exotic East. Pictures of women in Turkish baths appeared and stories of harems multiplied.

All this has now begun to change. Instead of the hostility and superiority which has been our attitude for so long, there is now a real attempt to understand. Recently a group of Jews, Christians and Muslims went together to Jordan. A Rabbi friend on that trip wrote to me this week to say 'enormous strides have been made since the first time this group met in 1984.' In a number of places now in this country and abroad small Abrahamic groups are setting up – groups of people from all three of the religions that regard themselves as in some sense spiritual descendants of Abraham. Scholars have long appreciated the contribution of Islam to European philosophy and science. Now many Christians are beginning to discover resonances in Islam to their own faith. For example, there is this little prayer from an Islamic source, which most Christians would be happy to use:

Praise be to him who, when I call on him,
Answers me, slow though I am when he calls me.
Praise be to him who gives to me when I ask him,
Miserly though I am when he asks a loan of me.
My Lord I praise, for he is of my praise most worth.

Of course, Prince Charles was right that there is still a great deal of work to be done in breaking down prejudices. And there is an ugly side to Islam in some places, as there is to Christianity. But if we are sometimes tempted to get gloomy and think that human history is simply a tale of things going from bad to worse, we should reflect that in our relationship with Islam there has been a real change for the better. After 1300 years characterized by little more than fear and fascinated disdain, there is now the seed of understanding and appreciation.

BEARING THE HURT

27 March 1992

JUST SUPPOSE THAT YOU ARE LEFT SOME MONEY IN A WILL, and you decide to use it to help your children. Unfortunately one of them fritters his share away, his business gets into trouble and his house is at risk. You worry about whether you should scrape something together to bail him out. All your best parental instincts make you want to help, but part of you thinks it is important for him to learn a lesson, even if it is the hard way. Then, of course, there is the question of what is fair to your other children.

This is just one example of the tension between being kind and being fair, which faces us every day and which has been played out so publicly this week over Mike Tyson's prison sentence for rape. Now that he has been jailed for six years there will be sorrow, not just for him and his tragic fall, but also for the black community, for many of whom he has been a hero.

The Baptist Church in America has been calling for mercy, asking for a suspended sentence, but there are many thousands of women in the USA, of all colours, who have suffered sexual violence. They too need mercy. They are the prime victims whom society should be seeking to protect. However sad it may be, it is right that Tyson, having been found guilty, should be jailed. Justice needs to be done both for his own long-term good and for the protection of others. And yet justice cannot be the last word, or none of us would be able to rest easy.

All the great religions stress that at the heart of the universe there is mercy. 'The Lord is gracious, his mercy is everlasting', as Psalm 100 puts it. But this mercy cannot be a cheap option. It is not indifference or benign tolerance. So many of our actions have destructive consequences that have to be suffered by others. There is pain to be borne, and for Christians the cross of Christ is a sign of the hurt that God eternally bears in his heart as he seeks to bring us into relationship with himself and one another.

And if all this sounds rather grim, there is also hope – hope that despite the tragedy and hurt, relationships can ultimately be restored.

In Dostoevsky's great novel *The Brothers Karamazov* there is a discussion about heaven as a place of mutual forgiveness. Ivan protests against this, and argues that no heavenly harmony could justify the terrible suffering that many people endure in the world on their way to that harmony. So he hands back his ticket – God was not justified in creating us – the cost is too high. Point taken. But we *have* been created, and if there is to be any healing in life's sins and sorrows it can only be in a community characterized by mutual forgiveness. Jesus put it so simply and starkly when he taught us to pray, 'Father, forgive us our sins as we forgive those who sin against us.' Justice has to be done, for everyone's sake. But beyond justice we look for a society, rooted in the forgiveness of God, in which we offer that forgiveness to one another in all our failure and brokenness.

Not in Vain

19 March 1993

YESTERDAY WAS THE ONE HUNDREDTH ANNIVERSARY OF the birth of the poet Wilfred Owen – and a number of celebrations were held in different parts of the country. 'My subject is war,' he wrote, 'and the pity of war. The poetry is in the pity.' No other poet this century has so shaped the way we see things. Owen's poems are studied in almost every school in the country; they have been turned into memorable music by Benjamin Britten; they have brought about a fundamental shift of attitude. Quite simply, he has stripped war of all its false glamour. If today, as we hear the news of more killings, we are filled again with a sense of the pity of war – the waste, the futility – it is because the lines of Wilfred Owen have entered our very bones.

It's not as though we have all become pacifists. Most of us haven't. War may still sometimes be a last resort, when all else has failed, to avert a greater evil – but in such cases we see it as a tragic necessity, not as a great romantic endeavour or on occasion for heroics. Brave and honourable people still die in the cause of duty, as soldiers have done this week in Northern

Ireland; but we do not pretend that this is anything less than a terrible sadness.

The world today, with violence in every continent, looks no better than it did in the time of Owen. Yet, in part due to him, we desperately want the peacemakers to succeed – we want a settlement in Bosnia, in Israel, in South Africa and elsewhere; we want the hand of the United Nations to be strengthened – and it will need to be stronger still. Yet, even so, ever since Cain killed Abel, violence has been part of the scene, and it is difficult to think of a time, till Kingdom come, when it will be eliminated. There is an inescapable tragic dimension to life, and we need faith not only to firm up the forces of peace but to give us courage to go on when they fail.

Wilfred Owen began one poem with the words:

'O Jesus Christ!' one fellow sighed.
And kneeled, and bowed, tho' not in prayer, and died.
And the bullets sang 'In vain',
Machine guns chuckled 'Vain',
Big guns guffawed 'In Vain'.

It is easy to feel what Owen felt. So I also like to bear in mind the thought of Paul that our best endeavours are never wasted. 'Therefore, my beloved brethren,' he wrote, 'be steadfast, immovable, always abounding in the work of the Lord, knowing that in the Lord your labour is not in vain.'

SHARING THE TEARS

1 October 1993

WHEN I FIRST HEARD THE NEWS OF THE EARTHQUAKE IN India my immediate reaction was 'Where is it?' My son is working as a doctor there, so it was a relief to learn that the epicentre was many hundreds of miles away from where he is living. We think instinctively of ourselves and our families – and only slowly do we widen the circle of our concern to include others. It's difficult also to take in the intensity of the suffering. There is a world of difference between being there as one of the bereaved or injured and trying to imagine their plight.

There's another problem too. We hear about so many tragedies and disasters. If we let ourselves feel even a fraction of this mountain of pain we would soon be crushed. In order to survive at all, we have to block out most human anguish. Yet, in order to survive as human beings, we must let some in.

In the trenches of the First World War, Wilfred Owen partly envied those who could shut out the terrible carnage around them. He begins one poem by praising those who cease to feel. But in the last verse he revolts against this insensibility. Cursed are those who 'make themselves like stones', he wrote, 'wretched are they and mean'.

By choice they made themselves immune
to pity and whatever mourns in man...
Whatever mourns when many leave these shores;
whatever shares
The eternal reciprocity of tears.

To be human, to remain human, means allowing ourselves to feel something, however small, of what others feel. In the parable of the Good Samaritan those who walked by on the other side were good, upright people. But they lacked imagination. They could not widen their sympathy to encompass the one who was lying in the road. Lazarus was at the door of Dives every day, but Dives could not see him – that is, see him as someone like himself.

Faced with disasters of this magnitude, there is first the question: 'Is there anything I can do to help?' Earlier this year in Armenia I visited a wonderful new school built by British aid after an equally devastating earthquake. Local people and the Indian emergency services seem to be working well, but often there is something we can do, even if it is only giving money. For those of us who pray, there will be a helpless, confused kind of prayer, perhaps just 'O Lord, have mercy; O God, have pity.' But both action and prayer are rooted in a fundamental respect, in silence before the suffering of fellow human beings.

APPROACHING THE END

IN THE GLADNESS OF TODAY

8 May 1992

A MAN I KNEW MADE MONEY AND RETIRED, IN HIS EARLY forties, to a Greek island. He built himself a dream house on a dream site overlooking the sea, and there he stayed. I visited him 30 years later. The carpets were now fading, the house was in a state of disrepair. I wondered whether his long retirement in the sun had been such a good idea after all. As a life, what did it all add up to? I did not envy him.

This week various institutions concerned with our pensions are again debating the question of retirement age. Men and women should be allowed to retire on pension at the same age – or so I believe. But if we all retire at 60 it will cost the country a lot of money. On the other hand, if 65 is made the retirement age for all, then many women will feel disadvantaged. So, as we heard on the *Today* programme yesterday, 63 has been suggested as a compromise, cost-neutral age for both women and men.

I suspect that whatever age is finally decided on, we will continue to fantasize about retirement, about a life free of pressure, a life of leisure. Brute reality suggests something rather different.

For, first, retirement is a killer. Too often we hear the sad story of a couple who have longed and saved for retirement over many years, and then one of them, usually the husband, drops dead within a year. Perhaps years of strain and overwork have taken their toll. ·

Secondly, retirement brings many new problems. We may put behind us the demands of work, but there is, for example, the necessity to adjust to a new domestic routine. As a friend once remarked about her husband's retirement, 'For better, for worse, yes. For richer for poorer, yes. In sickness and in health, yes. Home for lunch every day, no.' There is no problem-free period in our lives. At every stage there are particular claims, demands and opportunities to respond to.

The implications seem quite clear. Don't look to a golden age in the future any more than to a golden age in the past. Now is the time to improve the quality of our life.

In John's Gospel it is recorded that a friend of Jesus called Lazarus died. Lazarus's sister Martha said to Jesus, 'I know that he will rise again at the resurrection of the last day.' Jesus responded with those amazing, haunting words: 'I am the resurrection and the life', words always read at funerals. But their point in John's Gospel is that resurrection to true life, to new life, takes place now. Martha looked to the future for physical resurrection. Jesus replied that he has brought the future near, into the present. He brings spiritual renewal, raises us now into the eternal now.

Retirement can be a real blessing, a wonderful gift of God. But we can't count on it. And whatever the Government eventually decides about pensions, it is the quality of life now that matters. And this, as the Christian community at Taizé in France puts it, is about living 'in the gladness of today'.

An Unthanked Old Man

21 July 1997

THERE ARE REPORTS FROM AMERICA OF GRANNIES BEING wheeled into supermarkets and simply abandoned. A play has even been written about this called *Granny Dumping*. I was with some friends of my own age over the weekend, and we were joking about this disturbing phenomenon, speculating on which supermarket we would rather be left in. Sainsbury's might offer some air miles for a last fling, but no doubt Waitrose and Tesco's would have something to offer as well. More seriously, the question of how old people are going to be looked after is now a major problem, not only here and in America but also, I understand, in countries that have traditionally respected old age, such as Malaysia.

Some of those who are tempted to jettison their aged relatives are under terrible pressure. I heard of one home in which an aged mother was being looked after, where the husband said to his wife one day, 'Either she goes or I go.' And it's not only aged relatives, of course. Some of the most heroic people in our society are those who day after day look after their handicapped children. As a society we need to offer such carers all

121

the help we can. In the vast majority of situations the care is there – but it does need to be supported.

Sometimes that care is present in the most surprising people. Les Murray's latest collection of poems contains one entitled 'Australian Love Poem'. It's about a teacher who perhaps gets too fond of his female pupils and so has to move on. He comes to lodge with a couple whose only interests in life seem to be cards, horses and malicious gossip. Then the husband dies and the lodger looks after his widow. The poem ends:

As she got lost in the years
where she would wander
her boy would hold her in bed
and wash sheets to be spread under.

But when her relations carried her,
murmuring, out to their van,
he fled that day, as one with no rights,
as an unthanked old man.

It's difficult to think of a more unpromising subject than that old man. Understandably, the relatives ignored him. But Les Murray, like all good poets, opens our eyes to see what normally we pass by. In very practical ways – washing the sheets – he has cared for the old lady. According to the Christian version of what it is to be a human being, within all of us, however covered, there is a capacity to care. And Jesus, the one who indeed opens our eyes, seemed to find it in the most unlikely people.

ACCOMPANYING THE DYING

9 July 1993

WE ARE SO USED TO NEWS ABOUT DIVISION AND DIFFER-
ences of opinion in the Church that it is good to hear about
agreement for a change. Yesterday Roman Catholic and Church
of England Bishops issued a joint statement, endorsed by the
Free Churches, on euthanasia. Quite simply, all the churches
agree that the law should not be changed to allow for voluntary
euthanasia. Life is a gift of God and it is wrong, even when old
and decrepit, to kill oneself or to persuade others to do so.

My mother had a severe stroke from which she never
recovered. She could not walk; worse, she could not speak. For
three years she was in anguish; and her family and friends felt
with her and for her. Yet it never occurred to any of us to end
her daily struggle with an injection. This was, I think, because
we still wanted her with us; and she wanted to be with us. If
someone asks to be put out of their misery, and we agree to
their request, it must inevitably be interpreted in part as a kind
of not wanting that person, a pushing away, a rejection.

People do sometimes find life a terrible burden. A bishop
friend of mine tells of an old man who felt like this and on

more than one occasion asked to be given a pill so that he could, as he put it, 'just float away'. Yet on each occasion, half an hour later he said, 'Don't take any notice of me. I'm just a silly old man.' If the law allowed for voluntary euthanasia the trust between that man and his doctor would be undermined. A person could be made to feel such a nuisance that they would feel that they had no option but to ask to die, to spare others the burden of caring for them.

Rejecting euthanasia does not mean, in the words of the poet Clough, that we have to strive officiously to keep someone alive. On the contrary, there comes a point when it is absolutely right just to let them die; and the churches have always made it quite clear that we have a moral right to refuse burdensome treatment. But there is a crucial moral distinction between killing someone and letting them die; between administering a poison the sole purpose of which is to kill, and giving, for example, a large dose of morphine, which relieves suffering but which also has the effect of shortening life. The latter is simply good medical practice. We do not want a law that would blunt that distinction. What we do need is the highest standard of terminal care, not just in hospices but in every hospital and home. For however old and frail we may be, each one of us is an eternal soul – and, as Jesus so vividly put it, every hair on our head is numbered. What the elderly or dying do want is our friendship and companionship, whereby we convey to them the sense that they are not alone. We are with them; and through our presence, God is with them.

LAST WORDS

23 December 1994

LATER TODAY I WILL BE GOING TO THE FUNERAL OF PETER Hebblethwaite, a distinguished Catholic journalist. A former priest and Jesuit, he was one of a number of able men who left the priesthood in recent decades and who married. He wrote major biographies of two modern popes, as well as being a sharp commentator on church affairs. His health was not good, and when he was taken ill in the middle of a TV programme recently, he was heard rehearsing his last words: 'I love my wife. I love my children. I love the Society of Jesus' – words which I find wonderfully moving.

Last words seem to fall into three main categories. There are those which come from people who are facing the executioner and are trying to put a brave face on it – for example, Thomas More's words when he ascended the scaffold: 'See me safe up; for my coming down, let me shift for myself.' As one would expect, there are devout last words. Innumerable people, famous and unknown, have died with the words of Jesus on their lips, 'Father, into thy hands I commit my spirit.' Then there are those words which are utterly characteristic of a person's whole life and outlook, like Cecil Rhodes': 'So little done, so much to do.' One of my favourite characters is the eighteenth-century traveller and letter writer, Lady Mary Wortley Montague. Her last words, 'It has all been very interesting', perfectly catch her aristocratic zest for life.

A good number of last sayings are rather portentous, as though the speaker, or their followers who polished the words, wanted something noble to go down in history, which is why I prefer those with a bit of a tease about them. One of my favourite stories concerns a sage who was dying. His followers gathered from all round the world to hear his dying utterance: 'Life,' they heard him say, 'is a glass of wine.' In fact the sage didn't die immediately, and his followers dispersed to their homes, puzzling away and asking others what this meant. A few months later they were again called to his bedside and they pressed him for the meaning which had eluded them. 'Ah well,' he replied, 'life is not a glass of wine,' and expired.

It is this element of tease, of a surface playfulness hiding a deeper seriousness, that I like about Peter Hebblethwaite's words. A former Jesuit, a soldier in the celibate army of God, saying both 'I love my wife. I love my children' and that he loved the Jesuits. But he did not actually use the word 'Jesuit'. In the phrase he did use, 'I love the Society of Jesus', there is a glimpse of the depths – of that society, that company, that accompanying and companionship with Jesus, which death cannot destroy.

A TIME TO DIE

18 February 1994

TO THE OLD LIFE CAN SEEM BURDENSOME, PARTICULARLY IF they are in discomfort. Sensitive people can also feel that they are a burden to others, especially if they know that they need a lot of looking after. And it is all too easy to imagine the effect that allowing euthanasia would have on them: 'I'm more and more bother to others. Perhaps I'd better ask the doctor to give me a pill to take me off their hands.' The effect on some of those who have to care for the long-term sick could be as bad: the temptation to get them to ask for that pill or injection – or, even worse, the fear that this is what the patient suspects you think. Then there is the pressure exerted by scarce resources: a ward full of senile old people, with a great queue outside of others wanting a bed.

So, thank goodness, the House of Lords Select Committee on Medical Ethics, which reported yesterday, came out decisively against changing the law to permit euthanasia. We are still a civilized country. That fundamental trust which needs to exist between patient and doctor and family will remain in place. It won't be undermined by a nagging doubt that the doctor is about to suggest a life-ending injection or that other people would really like me to ask for one.

This does not mean, as the report makes clear, that we have to strive to stay alive at all costs. We have a right to refuse treatment. As the Pope put it in his *Declaration on Euthanasia* a few years back, 'When inevitable death is imminent it is permitted in conscience to take the decision to refuse forms of treatment that would only secure a precarious and burdensome prolongation of life.' Or, as the Book of Ecclesiastes says, 'For everything there is a season ... a time to be born and a time to die.'

When my time comes to go I don't want endless treatment; I want just to be free of pain, comfortable and supported by family and friends. So I'm glad that yesterday's report also recommends support for research into pain, and the development of palliative care in hospices, hospitals and the community, as well as special regard to the maintenance of individual dignity for those in long-term care.

I also want to be spiritually sustained by the prayers of good people. A couplet in one of Charles Wesley's great hymns always gets me pondering. It prays that our lives might show faith and love:

Till death thy endless mercies seal
And make my sacrifice complete

It implies that death, as part of nature, at the proper time, is within the providence of God; and that a life offered to God and others in love can find its proper culmination at the end. And I think especially of the last prayer of Jesus, 'Father, into thy hands I commit my spirit.'

Not a usual way of looking at death these days, or an easy one. But I find it a hopeful ideal for which to aim.

LIGHT IN OUR DARKNESS

18 December 1992

THE WORLD SEEMS TO BE SUCH A GHASTLY MESS AT THE moment that I would love to be able to say something cheerful this morning. But it's difficult to be hopeful without appearing to ignore the tragedies all about us, so I will begin with a seemingly sad story – it's printed in the Christmas edition of the Oxford Diocesan newspaper. The editor had asked three people to say how their life had changed in 1992.

One man described life with his wife, who suffered from clinical depression, and how he couldn't handle it. Then, even worse, she got cancer. But as this spread, suddenly everything changed. As he wrote:

Life became so precious a gift, each moment offered even more chance to be healed. The cancer was a body problem: healing was at a much deeper level in the spirit. The last months became an extraordinary joy.

His wife came to death with a great sense of assurance and faith. It felt, he said, 'Like a very holy thing, as though we were surrounded by angels.'

The hope that we have is not just for eternal life – though this, I believe, is real; we have hope so that even in our darkest moments, light can shine. And sometimes, the deeper the darkness is, the more we can both see and reveal that light. For that man and his wife things became both worse and better at the same time.

The famous scholar of English literature, F. R. Leavis, once tried to puzzle out why it is that, when we watch a tragedy on the stage, far from feeling depressed, we enjoy a sense of enhanced vitality. He came to the conclusion that it is because tragedy, as he put it, 'involves recognizing a positive value as in some way defined and vindicated by death'. The value of what is destroyed is somehow brought into sight only by the destruction. Certainly, this was true for the first Christians. They saw in the death of Christ not just the terrible destruction of life but the revelation of true life, of life lived totally at one with God. So they could write of that cruel torture as at the same time being a revelation of the human/divine glory – which lies latent in us all.

We can't deny that things are bleak at the moment, and those who are among the nearly three million unemployed will be feeling this in a very personal way. But I'm not going to run through a catalogue of the world's woes again. Just because things are so black, the good that we do today will shine out that much more clearly. Even if we don't succeed very well, even if we fail, the darkness will not overcome it.

THE DEATH OF A PRINCESS

31 August 1997

AT A TIME LIKE THIS WE ALL REACH FOR THE SAME INAD-equate words. We have a sense of shock, of deep sadness, especially for the two princes – young boys who have lost their mother so suddenly. The prayers of all who pray will be with them today.

Princess Diana was the best known, the most sought after, the most photographed figure in the world, combining the glamour of a superstar with the aura of royalty and her own personal magnetism. But in the end, like each one of us, she was a person with her own thoughts and struggles, her own hopes and despairs.

The real Diana, who, despite the media attention and even the friendship of her closest friends, was someone whom only she really knew – that inner person, with the scars left by her own parents' divorce, her struggles to overcome bulimia, her unhappy marriage. How tempting it must have been for her to just not bother, to give up, to despair. But instead she made something of her life, emerging as a person in her own right –

above all drawing on the well of her own suffering to feel for others who were in pain.

Few of us are fully aware of why we do what we do or of the range of motives that drive us. But the simple fact is that Princess Diana reached out from her own vulnerability to those in distress – to those suffering from AIDS, to children mutilated by mines – willing to touch, hold and hug both young and old. That, in a cold and cynical world, is something for which we should be profoundly thankful.

In her inner struggles it was clear too that the Princess was trying to make sense of life, trying to find some meaning and purpose in it all. How far she got I don't know. But I do know that the God to whom she goes is good and just and gentle. He is a God who knows her better than she knew herself, who desires her wellbeing more passionately than she desired it herself. That is why, like many other Christians, I want to pray, 'Rest eternal, grant unto them, O Lord; let life perpetual shine upon them' for her and for the others who were killed in the car crash. For as St Paul wrote, 'I am sure that neither death, nor life, nor things present, nor things to come, nor anything else in all creation, will be able to separate us from the love of God in Christ Jesus our Lord.'

The fairy story has turned into a Greek tragedy. There is an inescapable tragic element to human existence. But through the cross and resurrection of Christ, tragedy does not have to be the last word. We commend her to a faithful God.

A FATHER'S DEATH

19 October 1991

LATER TODAY I WILL BE ATTENDING THE FUNERAL OF MY father, who died early on Monday morning. The death of a parent, however expected, at however advanced an age, always leaves a great gap; and, of course, this is an experience we all have to go through.

Dylan Thomas, writing at the death of his father, said that old age should always 'Rage, rage against the dying of the light.' This is a view that has often been expressed in the twentieth century, notably by Simone de Beauvoir when her mother died. She held that whenever death comes it is 'an untimely violence'. Sadly, it too often is, as it was for those poor people who were killed in Texas recently when the gunman ran amok, as it will be for those who will be shot in Northern Ireland or killed on the roads today. But not all deaths are like that. My father was 91, had lived a full life through momentous times, and had been loved by family and friends. In his last years he had been well looked after by my sister and her husband. He read much in the mystics, especially Eckhart. He told me of at least two occasions recently when he had experienced extraordinary peace and blessedness, when a long passage of time passed without him noticing it. We ought not to over-emphasize the importance of religious experiences, because they depend on so many factors, but there is no doubt that my father was left with a sense of serenity for days afterwards.

In short, he was prepared and ready to go. I think of the story in Luke's Gospel of the aged Simeon waiting in the temple. On seeing the Christ child he uttered those wonderful words: 'Lord, now lettest thou thy servant depart in peace; for mine eyes have seen thy salvation.'

People used to speak of making a good death, one in which we are at peace with ourselves, with other people and with God. It would be a pity if the idea got altogether lost.

For there is work to be done in our last years, which might involve the laying aside of resentments, the making up of old quarrels, drawing closer to those around us, facing up to that mixture of confused and painful feelings that most of us carry around inside; and, through it all, a learning to live in the presence of God and to wait upon him. That is why the old Prayer Book Litany prays that we might be delivered from 'battle, murder and sudden death'. We need time at the end.

I will miss the weekly telephone calls to my father, his little list of things he always kept to talk about – for he was a well-organized man to the last – his frank comments about my latest 'Thought for the Day'. But I am deeply grateful that he went in peace. In a world so full of untimely death, unhappiness and spiritual emptiness, his end-time was a blessing that I would wish for myself and all of us.

THE MUSIC WHICH IS ME
IN THE HEART OF GOD

24 June 1994

MY MOTHER WAS AN ECONOMICAL PERSON, SO AS A
teenager I had my father's cut-down tennis shorts. They were
rather baggy and I was glad to get rid of them a few years ago.
It seems I needn't have bothered. Like millions of others, I have
been watching a bit of Wimbledon, and have seen baggy shorts
back in fashion.

It was a particular delight yesterday to see Martina
Navratilova with her wonderful, flowing drives. Indeed, Harry
Williams once suggested that playing tennis on form is a kind
of foretaste of the Resurrection. So often we have an uneasy,
uncomfortable relationship with our bodies, but when we are
playing well, mind and body working in harmony, the old dualism is overcome and we are a 'total undivided self'.

Sadly, the Church has sometimes been guilty of dualism –
that is, of conveying a negative attitude to the body. But in
the Bible, our foundation document, bodily life is regarded as
something to be glad about. As Psalm 93 puts it: 'I will give
thanks unto thee, for I am fearfully and wonderfully made:
marvellous are thy works, and that my soul knoweth right

well.' Although my own tennis is not up to much these days, I can echo those words for someone like Agassi, as he brings off one of those unexpected, superbly controlled lobs that go right over the opponent's head and drop just inside the baseline.

Yet, the time is coming when even Martina Navratilova will no longer be playing at Wimbledon, and an even more melancholy time approaches when we will hardly have the strength to watch it, even on TV. With old age comes an inevitable bodily decline, even for the Joan Hunter Dunn of Betjeman's poem, 'furnished and burnished by Aldershot Sun'. The question then, is what about the soul – the immortal soul? Such words are, of course, philosophically very tricky, and I prefer to look at them from a slightly different angle. My soul, my true self, however unknown to me, is known to God. Whatever happens when I close my eyes in death, the person I truly am is known to God, and his knowledge of me does not cease.

There comes a time when there is no earthly instrument, no earthly score, but the music which is me remains in the heart of God. He can play it again, if he wills, on another instrument, in a manner and form appropriate to an eternal orchestra.

The grace of a well-hit ball is a sign of a person at one with themselves, body and mind working in harmony. But this itself points to the desirability of a profounder unity still – a unity of all that we are, body, mind and spirit, with the fount from whom our being flows.

ACKNOWLEDGEMENTS

The Editor and Publishers are grateful for permission to use the following material, which is reproduced by permission of the copyright holders:

pp. 9–10, 124: extracts from 'The Quality of Sprawl' and 'Australian Love Poem', both by Les Murray, from *Collected Poems*, Carcenet Press, 1998.

pp. 16–17: extract from 'In a Bath Tea-shop' by John Betjeman, from *Collected Poems*, John Murray (Publishers) Ltd, 1979.

p. 24: extracts from 'Flute-Music' by Rabindranath Tagore, translated by William Radice, from *Selected Poems*, Penguin, 1985, © William Radice, 1985.

Also by Richard Harries

Prayers of Hope, Mowbrays, 1975

Turning to Prayer, Mowbrays, 1978

Prayers of Grief and Glory, Lutterworth, 1979

Being a Christian, Mowbrays, 1981

(also published in the USA as *What Christians Believe*,
   Winston Press, 1981)

Should a Christian Support Guerillas?, Lutterworth, 1979

Praying Round the Clock, Mowbrays, 1983

The Authority of Divine Love, Blackwells, 1983

Prayer and the Pursuit of Happiness, Collins, 1985

(also published in the USA, Eerdmans, 1985)

Morning Has Broken, Marshall Pickering, 1985

Christianity and War in a Nuclear Age, Mowbrays, 1986

C. S. Lewis: the Man and His God, Collins, 1987

Christ Is Risen, Mowbrays, 1988

*Is There a Gospel for the Rich? The Christian in a Capitalist
   World*, Mowbrays, 1992

Art and the Beauty of God, Mowbrays, 1993

The Real God, Mowbrays, 1994

Questioning Belief, SPCK, 1995

A Gallery of Reflections – The Nativity of Christ, Lion/BRF,
   1995

Seasons of the Spirit (with George Every and Kallistos Ware),
   SPCK, 1984

(also published in the USA as *The Time of the Spirit*, St
   Vladimir's Seminary Press, 1984)

The One Genius: Through the Year with Austin Farrer, SPCK,
   1987

Two Cheers for Secularism (with Sidney Brichto), Pilkington,
   1998

fireandwater
The book-lover's website

www.fireandwater.com

The latest news from the book world

Interviews with leading authors

Win great prizes every week

Join in lively discussions

Read exclusive sample chapters

Catalogue & ordering service

www.fireandwater.com
Brought to you by HarperCollins*Publishers*